Bootstrapping Your Business to Success

Building a Business Without VC

Harrell Howard

Table of Contents

Table of Contents	**2**
Introduction: The Power of Bootstrapping	**6**
Why write this book?	6
What bootstrapping means and how it differs from VC funding	8
Success stories of bootstrapped businesses	10
What you'll learn from this book	12
Chapter 1: The Mindset of a Bootstrapper	**15**
Chapter 2: Choosing the Right Business Idea	**23**
Start with your skills and experience	24
Look for real market demand	25
Choose an idea you're passionate about	28
Bootstrapping ideas in action	32
Chapter 3: Planning for Success with a Lean Business Plan and Clear Goals	**35**
Crafting a lean business plan	36
Setting clear, achievable goals	40
Tools for planning and goal-setting	42
The importance of flexibility and iteration	44
Chapter 4: Funding Your Business Without VC	**47**
Personal savings and credit cards	47
Friends and family rounds	49
Crowdfunding	51
Grants and pitch competitions	52
Customer funding and pre-sales	54
Bootstrapper-friendly loans and financing	56
Parting thoughts	58
Chapter 5: Building a Minimum Viable Product (MVP) with Limited Resources	**60**
Define your core value proposition	61
Identify your riskiest assumptions	62
Prioritize features ruthlessly	65

Leverage existing tools and platforms	67
Prioritize speed over perfection	69
Measure and iterate	71
Final Thought on Building MVP	74

Chapter 6: Marketing on a Budget: Grassroots Strategies, Social Media, and Networking — 76

Leverage your personal network	76
Tap into online communities	78
Create valuable content	80
Leverage social media	83
Partner with influencers and thought leaders	85
Guest blogging or podcast appearances	86
Get creative with guerrilla marketing	87
Measure and optimize your efforts	89
Final Thought on Marketing on a Budget	91

Chapter 7: Generating Revenue Early: Pre-Sales, Subscriptions, and Multiple Revenue Streams — 93

Pre-sell your product before it's built	94
Offer a subscription or recurring revenue model	96
Develop multiple revenue streams	98
Price your product effectively	101
Test and adapt over time	104
Final Thought	106

Chapter 8: Operating Lean: Keeping Costs Low, Outsourcing, and Managing Cash Flow — 108

Keep your fixed costs low	108
Outsource non-core functions	110
Manage your cash flow carefully	112
Leverage automation and technology	114
Foster a culture of frugality and resourcefulness	117
Final Thought	119

Chapter 9: Building a Small but Mighty Team and Creating a Strong Culture — 121

    Hire for fit and potential — 121
    Onboard and train effectively — 124
    Foster a culture of transparency and communication — 126
    Empower and trust your team — 127
    Invest in employee development and growth — 130
    Final Thought — 131

Chapter 10: Dealing with Setbacks and Pivoting When Necessary — 133
    Embrace a growth mindset — 133
    Conduct a post-mortem analysis — 135
    Be willing to pivot when necessary — 137
    Build resilience through adversity — 140
    Final Thought — 142

Chapter 11: Competing with VC-Backed Companies by Focusing on Customer Loyalty and Sustainable Growth — 144
    Focus on customer loyalty and retention — 145
    Emphasize sustainable growth and profitability — 147
    Differentiate through unique value proposition and customer experience — 149
    Leverage agility and adaptability — 152
    Final Thought — 154

Chapter 12: Avoiding Burnout and Maintaining Balance — 156
    Recognize the signs of burnout — 156
    Set realistic expectations and boundaries — 158
    Prioritize self-care and stress management — 159
    Cultivate a supportive network and seek help when needed — 161
    Celebrate successes and milestones along the way — 164
    Final Thought — 166

Chapter 13: Growing Sustainably by Reinvesting Profits and Scaling Responsibly — 168
    Reinvest profits into the business — 168
    Scale responsibly and strategically — 171
    Balance growth with profitability — 174
    Plan for the long term — 176

Final Thought	179

Chapter 14: Staying True to Your Vision and Building a Legacy Business 181

Define your purpose and values	182
Communicate and embed your purpose and values	183
Focus on creating value, not just wealth	186
Build a strong and sustainable culture	**187**
Plan for succession and continuity	190
Final Thought	192
Conclusion	**194**
Appendices	**200**
Tools:	200
Case Studies of Successful Bootstrapped Businesses	201
Templates for Lean Business Planning and Budgeting	203
1. Problem	203
2. Solution	203
3. Key Metrics	203
4. Unique Value Proposition	203
5. Unfair Advantage	203
6. Channels	204
7. Customer Segments	204
8. Cost Structure	204
9. Revenue Streams	204
Budget Template:	205
Explanation of the Table:	207

Introduction: The Power of Bootstrapping

Why write this book?

When we talk of startups and entrepreneurship, it's easy to get caught up in the allure of venture capital funding. We've all heard the success stories of companies that raised millions from VCs and went on to become household names. But what these headlines often fail to mention is that the vast majority of successful businesses are actually built without any VC money at all. They're bootstrapped - funded by the founders' own savings, revenue from early customers, and sheer determination.

I was inspired to write this book because I believe bootstrapping is an underrated but incredibly powerful approach to building a business. When you bootstrap, you retain full control over your company's vision and direction. You're not beholden to the demands of outside investors or the pressure to grow at all costs. Instead, you can focus on serving your customers, building a sustainable business model, and creating something you truly believe in.

Bootstrapping also forces you to be scrappy, resourceful and disciplined. Without a big injection of VC cash, you have to get creative about how you allocate resources, acquire customers, and generate revenue. This constraint can actually be a blessing in disguise, as it pushes you to validate your business idea early, stay lean and agile, and only spend money on what truly matters.

My goal with this book is to show you that bootstrapping is not just a viable path to building a successful business - in many cases, it's actually the best path. I'll walk you through the key principles and strategies used by successful bootstrappers, share inspiring case studies and examples, and give you a practical playbook for applying these lessons to your own entrepreneurial journey. Whether you're a first-time founder just starting out or an experienced entrepreneur looking to break free from the VC treadmill, this book will equip you with the mindset and tools you need to bootstrap your way to success.

What bootstrapping means and how it differs from VC funding

At its core, bootstrapping simply means funding your business through your own personal savings, early revenue from customers, and other non-VC sources like loans or grants. Instead of raising a big round of outside capital to get started, you use your own limited resources to get your idea off the ground and only spend money that you actually have.

This approach is fundamentally different from the VC model, where startups aim to raise increasingly larger rounds of funding to fuel rapid growth. With VC backing, the goal is usually to spend aggressively to acquire customers and capture market share, even if that means operating at a loss. The hope is that you'll eventually figure out a business model and become profitable, but the primary focus is on growth at all costs.

Bootstrapping flips this model on its head. Instead of optimizing for growth, you optimize for profitability and sustainability from the very beginning. You start small, get your product into the hands of paying customers as quickly as possible, and use that early revenue to slowly grow the business. Profitability is the goal from day one, not something to figure out later down the line.

This doesn't mean bootstrapped businesses can't grow quickly or reach significant scale. Many of the most successful bootstrapped companies like MailChimp and Basecamp have tens of millions in annual revenue. But they got there through steady organic growth driven by real customer demand, not artificial growth juiced by VC dollars.

The key distinction is that bootstrappers are focused on building real, sustainable businesses that generate profits and serve the needs of their customers. They grow more slowly and deliberately, which may not make for sexy headlines, but does create enduring companies built for the long-term. Bootstrapping is about creating a business that can thrive without being dependent on the constant infusion of outside cash.

Success stories of bootstrapped businesses

To illustrate the power of bootstrapping, let's look at a few noteworthy examples of companies that made it big without VC funding:

Mailchimp: This email marketing platform was started in 2001 by Ben Chestnut and Dan Kurzius as a side project to help their web design clients with email newsletters. They took no outside funding, charged customers from day one, and grew slowly by reinvesting profits. Today, Mailchimp has over $700M in annual revenue, was acquired for $12 billion in 2021, and is used by millions of businesses worldwide.

Basecamp: Formerly known as 37signals, Basecamp was founded by Jason Fried and David Heinemeier Hansson in 1999. They bootstrapped the company through web design consulting projects, eventually using the profits to develop their own project management software. Today Basecamp is used by millions and generates over $100M per year in revenue, having taken no venture funding in its 20+ year history.

Spanx: Sara Blakely famously started her shapewear company with just $5,000 of her own savings. She bootstrapped the business for years, only taking outside funding once the company was already highly profitable and generating tens of millions in annual revenue. Spanx was valued at $1.2 billion in 2021 when Blackstone acquired a majority stake.

Mojang: The Swedish video game studio behind Minecraft was bootstrapped by founder Marcus Persson, who funded the business through early sales of the game. Minecraft went on to be a worldwide phenomenon and cultural icon, leading to Microsoft acquiring Mojang for $2.5 billion in 2014.

Braintree: This payment processing startup was bootstrapped for its first few years, only raising its first round of funding after hitting $10M in revenue. It sold to PayPal for $800M in 2013.

These are just a few examples, but they underscore a powerful point - you don't need VC money to build an incredibly successful business. With the right product, business model and execution, it's entirely possible to bootstrap your way to a highly profitable, fast-growing and industry-leading company. Don't let the hype around VC funding make you think that's the only path to startup success.

What you'll learn from this book

My aim with this book is to give you a comprehensive, actionable guide to bootstrapping your own business from scratch. We'll dive deep into the key decisions, strategies and principles that separate successful bootstrappers from the rest. Specifically, you'll learn:

- The fundamentals of the bootstrapping mindset and how to cultivate key traits like resourcefulness, resilience and financial discipline
- Proven strategies for finding the right business idea and validating it quickly without spending a lot of money
- How to create a lean business plan and set clear, achievable goals to guide your bootstrapping journey

- The best ways to fund your business without VC money, from tapping your own savings to raising money from customers, grants and crowdfunding
- Tactics for building a minimum viable product (MVP) and getting it to market fast so you can start learning from real customers
- Scrappy, effective marketing approaches to help you find your first customers and start generating revenue
- Operational frameworks for keeping costs low, managing your cash flow, and optimizing for profitability
- Principled approaches to building a strong team and culture that will endure for the long haul
- Mental models for overcoming the inevitable challenges and setbacks you'll face while bootstrapping
- Guidance on how to scale sensibly, grow sustainably and stay true to your values as your business takes off

Perhaps most importantly, this book will give you confidence and inspiration to take the bootstrapping path. You'll read case studies of hugely successful bootstrapped companies across different industries, proving that this approach works. You'll see that you don't need special skills, a huge network or a groundbreaking idea - you just need to commit to the grind and hustle required to bootstrap.

By the end of this book, you'll have both the big picture vision and the nitty-gritty tactics needed to bootstrap your business. If you put these principles into action, stay disciplined and don't give up, you'll be well on your way to creating something you're truly proud of, just like the bootstrapping heroes that came before you. Let's dive in.

Chapter 1: The Mindset of a Bootstrapper

Before we dive into the tactics and strategies of bootstrapping, we need to talk about mindset. Because the truth is, successfully bootstrapping a business is as much about how you think as it is about what you do. The bootstrapping path is challenging - you'll face resource constraints, rejection from customers, doubt from friends and family, and constant pressure to make ends meet. To persevere and thrive in the face of these obstacles, you need to cultivate a particular way of thinking.

In my experience, successful bootstrappers tend to share a few key mental traits and philosophies:

Relentless resourcefulness: Bootstrappers view constraints as a creative challenge, not a dead end. They're masters at finding clever ways to solve problems, get things done and move forward with the limited resources at their disposal. Whether it's bartering services, repurposing old equipment, or negotiating deals, bootstrappers always look for scrappy solutions. They don't assume the way things have always been done is the only way.

Extreme ownership: When you're bootstrapping, there's no one else to blame for failures or challenges. Successful bootstrappers take complete responsibility for the outcomes of their business. They don't make excuses, and they don't wait for someone else to give them permission or resources. If something isn't working, they own it and fix it. This level of accountability can be daunting, but it's also deeply empowering.

Comfort with uncertainty: Bootstrapping a business is an inherently uncertain undertaking. You don't know if your idea will work, if customers will pay, if you'll be able to pay yourself a salary. There are no guarantees and no safety nets - which is very different from taking VC money or having a predictable day job. Bootstrappers have to get comfortable operating in the face of doubt and ambiguity. They focus on controlling what they can control and make peace with the rest.

Default to action: Because they have limited runway and resources, bootstrappers can't afford to get stuck in analysis paralysis or endless debates. They have a strong bias toward action, experimentation and getting things done. Even if the path ahead is uncertain, they choose to act and iterate rather than wait for perfect information. They subscribe to writer Grace Hopper's philosophy: "It's easier to ask forgiveness than it is to get permission."

Goal-oriented flexibility: Successful bootstrappers have a clarity of vision and strong internal compass. They know the ultimate destination they want to reach. But they balance this long-term orientation with short-term flexibility. As they encounter challenges and learn new information, they readily adapt their plans. They care more about achieving their goal than sticking to a pre-set route for getting there. This allows them to nimbly navigate obstacles without losing sight of the bigger picture.

Customer centricity: No business can succeed without happy customers, but this is especially true for bootstrapped startups. With a limited budget for marketing and sales, your product has to speak for itself and generate strong word-of-mouth. From day one, bootstrappers put their customers at the center of every decision. They obsess over understanding customers' needs, excelling at customer service, and going above-and-beyond to create a delightful user experience. This customer-centric approach helps the business punch above its weight.

Patience and persistence: Overnight successes are rare in the startup world, and they essentially don't exist for bootstrapped businesses. Bootstrapping is a marathon, not a sprint. It requires an incredible amount of persistence, patience and grit to build something from nothing. Successful bootstrappers are able to take the long view and not get discouraged by setbacks. They simply keep putting one foot in front of the other, no matter what obstacles come their way.

Intrinsic motivation: Bootstrapping a business is extremely hard, and the financial rewards aren't always certain. To persist through the ups and downs, you have to be fueled by intrinsic motivation. Successful bootstrappers are driven by a genuine passion for what they're building, a deep commitment to their team, and a desire to prove something to themselves. Of course, they want to make money and have a big exit, but those are secondary motivators. The real fire comes from within.

These traits form the core of the bootstrapping mindset. They're not just "nice to haves" - they're essential for navigating the challenges of starting and scaling a company without outside funding.

The good news is that these attitudes can be cultivated and strengthened like any skill or muscle. Even if you don't feel like you naturally embody all these traits today, you can develop them over time through practice and perseverance.

Here are a few concrete ways to start training your bootstrapping mindset:

Reframe challenges as opportunities

The next time you face a constraint or roadblock, ask yourself: "How could this help me? What creative solution is this forcing me to find?" Actively look for the opportunity in every challenge.

Build your tolerance for discomfort

Bootstrapping means getting used to living outside your comfort zone - whether that's cold calling customers, learning to code, or pitching investors. Lean into that discomfort and remind yourself it's a sign you're growing.

Celebrate small wins.

The bootstrapping journey is long and progress can feel slow. Make a point to celebrate the small milestones along the way - your first paying customer, your first hire, breaking even. Those little wins will give you fuel to keep going.

Find a community of like-minded founders

Surrounding yourself with other entrepreneurs who are in the trenches of building businesses can give you inspiration, emotional support, and practical advice.

Consider joining a startup incubator, attending founder meetups, or starting a mastermind group.

Define your "why."

Get crystal clear on why you're embarking on this entrepreneurial path. What's driving you, beyond just making money? The stronger your underlying purpose, the more likely you are to persist. Write it down and revisit it when you're facing challenges.

Study the stories of successful bootstrappers

Read books and case studies about entrepreneurs who built thriving businesses without VC funding, like the founders of Mailchimp, Basecamp, Spanx and others. Analyzing their journeys will give you mental models and inspiration for your own.

Remember, cultivating the bootstrapping mindset is a practice, not a destination. You'll have days when you feel invincible and days when you want to quit. The key is to keep showing up, keep putting in the reps, and trust that your resilience and resourcefulness will grow over time.

No matter what happens, know that you're in good company. Some of the most iconic and respected businesses of our time were bootstrapped in their early days. With the right mindset and strategies, you can absolutely follow in their footsteps - and write your own bootstrapping success story.

Chapter 2: Choosing the Right Business Idea

One of the most common questions I get from aspiring bootstrappers is: "How do I come up with a good business idea?" And it's a great question. When you're bootstrapping, you can't afford to spend months or years pursuing an idea that turns out to be a dud. You need to zero in on an opportunity with real legs - something that solves a genuine problem for customers and has the potential to generate revenue quickly.

The good news is that finding a solid bootstrapping idea is more about following a proven process than having a flash of inspiration. In my experience, the best ideas sit at the intersection of three key factors:

Your skills and experience: What are you uniquely good at? What knowledge and capabilities do you bring to the table?

Market demand: Is there a hungry market of people actively looking for solutions to the problem you want to solve? Are they willing and able to pay for those solutions?

Your passion: Do you genuinely care about this problem and the people affected by it? Are you excited to work on this for the next 5-10 years?

Let's unpack each of these factors in more detail.

Start with your skills and experience

As a bootstrapper, your biggest asset is your own time and expertise. You want to choose an idea that allows you to leverage your existing skills and knowledge, so you can hit the ground running and avoid an expensive learning curve.

Take an inventory of your professional background, side projects, hobbies and areas of deep interest. What do you know better than the average person? What comes naturally to you? These are clues to the kinds of problems you're uniquely equipped to solve.

For example, if you're a software engineer with a passion for productivity hacks, you might consider building tools to help individuals and teams work more efficiently. If you're a marketer who geeks out about analytics, you could start an agency that specializes in data-driven growth strategies. The key is to find an idea that feels like a natural extension of what you're already good at.

Of course, this doesn't mean you can't acquire new skills along the way. Successful entrepreneurs are always learning and stretching themselves. But bootstrapping is not the time for a ground-up reinvention. You want to put yourself in a position to add value from day one.

Look for real market demand

It's not enough to come up with an idea that sounds cool to you. For your business to succeed, there needs to be a substantial group of people who actively want what you're offering and are willing to pay for it. In other words, you need market demand.

One common trap that bootstrappers fall into is assuming that if they personally experience a problem, it must be a massive untapped opportunity. But just because something is a problem for you doesn't mean it's a problem for others. As Y Combinator co-founder Paul Graham puts it: "The mistake is to assume that if you're having a problem, so must everyone else. And further to assume that because no one seems to be solving this problem, there must be no good solutions."

To gauge whether there's real market demand, you need to get out of your own head and talk to potential customers. Conduct informal interviews, run online surveys, hang out where your target audience congregates online. Ask questions like:

What are your biggest pain points and frustrations related to [problem area]?

How are you currently dealing with those challenges? What solutions have you tried?

If you could wave a magic wand, what would a perfect solution look like?

How much would you be willing to pay for something that solved [problem] for you?

You're looking for signs that people are actively searching for better solutions in your space and hitting dead ends. Bonus points if they're already spending time or money on subpar alternatives. That's a strong indicator of real market demand.

For example, when Mailchimp's founders first had the idea for an email marketing tool, they didn't just run with it right away. They were already running a web design agency, so they had a built-in focus group of small business customers. Co-founder Ben Chestnut sent a simple email asking clients about their email marketing needs and frustrations - and the response was overwhelming. Almost everyone replied saying they wanted a better, simpler way to send email newsletters. That was the founders' cue that they were onto something big.

In addition to customer interviews, look for online and offline watering holes related to your problem space. Are there popular blogs, forums, social media groups or meetups dedicated to the topic? How much engagement do you see? What patterns emerge in the kinds of questions people are asking and the solutions they're seeking? These are all valuable signals of market demand.

Finally, consider looking at keyword search volume for terms related to your idea. If tens of thousands of people are searching for "best XYZ software" or "how to solve ABC problem" each month, that's a promising sign. Just be sure to also look at the search results themselves. Are there already a ton of well-established players dominating the space? If so, you'll need to get very specific about how you differentiate yourself.

Choose an idea you're passionate about

Bootstrapping a business is a long and often arduous journey. There will be plenty of ups and downs, good days and bad days, moments of doubt and frustration. To make it through all of that and keep moving forward, you need to be deeply invested in the problem you're solving.

Passion is an overused word in the startup world, but it's hard to overstate its importance for bootstrappers. When you're self-funding a business, you don't have the luxury of just clocking in and clocking out. Your business will consume a huge portion of your life for years to come. If you don't genuinely care about what you're building, you'll struggle to put in the hard work required for success.

This is why it's so important to choose an idea that resonates with you on a deeper level. Maybe it's a problem you've experienced firsthand and always wished someone would fix. Maybe it's an industry you've been fascinated by for years. Maybe it's a mission that aligns with your values and the impact you want to have on the world. Whatever it is, it should be something that energizes and inspires you - even on the tough days.

When I interviewed Sara Blakely about the early days of building Spanx, she told me: "I had a deep conviction and I cared so much about the idea. I knew that I would never have forgiven myself if I didn't at least try. Even though there were such bleak moments where I had doubts, I kept coming back to that core belief in what I was doing." That unwavering conviction is what gave Sara the stamina to keep pushing through challenges and setbacks.

Now, this isn't to say you need to be in love with every aspect of your business. There will always be tasks and responsibilities that feel like a grind - that's just the nature of entrepreneurship. But you should feel a deep sense of purpose and commitment to the overarching problem you're solving. That north star will help you stay focused and motivated for the long haul.

Putting it all together

Ultimately, finding the right bootstrapping idea is an exercise in pattern recognition. By looking at the intersection of your skills, market demand and passions, you can identify opportunities that are well-suited for your unique situation.

One framework I like to use is called the "idea matrix." Draw a simple chart with "skills" along one axis and "passions" along the other. In each box of the grid, brainstorm ideas at the intersection of those two elements. For example, under "writing skills" and "passion for environmental sustainability", you might list ideas like:

Blog about zero-waste living

Write guides on how businesses can reduce their carbon footprint

Start a copywriting agency aimed at clean energy companies

Once you have your matrix filled out, start researching the level of demand for each idea. You can use the customer interview and online research tactics we discussed earlier. As you evaluate ideas, rule out the ones that seem oversaturated or too small a market. Highlight the ones that seem promising from both a demand and personal standpoint.

After going through this exercise, you should have a solid list of potential bootstrapping ideas to explore further. Remember, your goal at this stage is not to find the perfect idea, but rather to identify a few strong contenders to validate with real-world tests. We'll talk more about how to validate and refine your idea in the next chapter.

For now, focus on brainstorming possibilities that align with your skills, the needs of the market, and your interests. The more boxes an idea checks, the better. And don't edit yourself too much at this stage - sometimes the most compelling opportunities come from unexpected combinations.

Bootstrapping ideas in action

Let's look at a few examples of bootstrappers who chose ideas at the intersection of their skills, market demand and passion:

Lynda Weinman was a graphic design instructor who started putting her courses online in the mid 90s, when web-based education was still a novelty. She had a hunch that design professionals would value high-quality, on-demand training - and she was right. Her site, Lynda.com, grew into a massive library of creative and technical courses. The company was acquired by LinkedIn for $1.5 billion in 2015.

Gina Trapani was a programmer who started a blog called Lifehacker in the early 2000s, dedicated to sharing technology tips and productivity hacks. The site quickly gained a cult following among tech-savvy readers. Trapani's posts combined her coding skills, passion for tech and knack for writing in a way that resonated with a large audience.

ConvertKit founder Nathan Barry was a designer who started blogging and writing ebooks about design and marketing. Through that experience, he identified a need for more powerful email marketing tools aimed at creators like himself. He used his design skills and firsthand knowledge of the creator market to bootstrap ConvertKit into a major player in the space.

In each of these cases, the founders zeroed in on an idea that was squarely in their zone of genius. They weren't chasing random opportunities or jumping on bandwagons. They were building businesses that felt authentic to their interests and experiences - which gave them unique advantages in their respective markets.

Finding a bootstrapping idea that hits this sweet spot takes work. You may need to go through multiple iterations and dead ends before landing on something with real potential. But by staying attentive to the intersection of your skills, market needs and passion, you'll be well on your way to finding an idea worth betting on. Keep brainstorming, keep validating, and trust that the right opportunity will emerge.

Chapter 3: Planning for Success with a Lean Business Plan and Clear Goals

Once you've identified a promising bootstrapping idea, it's tempting to dive right into building and launching. But before you get too far ahead of yourself, it's important to put some structure and planning in place. Having a clear roadmap will help you stay focused, make better decisions, and avoid costly mistakes down the line.

Now, when I say "planning", I don't mean spending months writing a 50-page business plan. As a bootstrapper, you need to stay lean and agile, which means adopting a more streamlined approach to planning. Your goal should be to get just enough clarity and direction to move forward confidently, without getting bogged down in analysis paralysis.

In this chapter, we'll walk through how to create a lean business plan that covers the essential bases, while still leaving room for pivots and iteration. We'll also talk about setting clear, achievable goals to guide your bootstrapping journey and help you measure progress along the way.

Crafting a lean business plan

A traditional business plan often includes lengthy market research, detailed financial projections, and a rigid five-year roadmap. But in the fast-moving world of startups, much of that information is either speculative or likely to change. As renowned entrepreneur and investor Steve Blank puts it: "No business plan survives first contact with customers."

Instead of overplanning, your focus as a bootstrapper should be on getting clear on the key assumptions and risks underlying your business idea, so you can systematically test and validate them. You want to have a general sense of where you're headed, but hold those plans loosely and be ready to adjust based on real-world feedback.

With that in mind, here are the essential components to include in your lean business plan:

Problem and solution summary: In a few sentences, articulate the problem you're solving, for whom, and how your offering will uniquely address it. This is your high-level hypothesis - the core assumption you'll be testing.

Target market and customer segments: Get specific about who you're aiming to serve. What are the key characteristics and needs of your target customers? If there are distinct subgroups within your market, take time to flesh out those different segments.

Value proposition and positioning: What unique benefits will you deliver to customers? How will you position yourself relative to alternatives in the market? Your goal is to stake out a clear, defensible niche.

Minimum Viable Product (MVP): Describe the simplest version of your offering that will allow you to test your core assumptions with real users. Focus ruthlessly on the features that matter most to your target customers.

Pricing model: How will you make money? Will you charge a one-time fee, a recurring subscription, a usage-based rate? Tie your pricing back to the value you're providing and the norms in your market.

Marketing and sales strategy: What channels and tactics will you use to get the word out and acquire customers? Think in terms of what's achievable with limited time and resources.

Key metrics and milestones: Define the quantitative indicators you'll use to gauge traction and progress. These could include revenue, number of paying customers, churn rate, Net Promoter Score, or other relevant metrics. Set some initial targets to aim for.

Team and resources: Who's involved in bringing this idea to life? What skills and experience do they bring? What key roles or resources are you missing that you'll need to acquire?

Financials: Create a simple financial model that estimates your expenses, revenue, and cash flow for the next 12-18 months. Focus on the key drivers and assumptions, and aim for ballpark ranges rather than precise numbers.

Risks and unknowns: Make a list of the biggest risks and open questions facing your business. These could relate to market demand, competition, technology challenges, legal or regulatory issues, or other factors. Brainstorm potential ways to mitigate or test these risks.

Notice what's not included in this lean plan: detailed market sizing, competitive analysis, long-term financial projections, an org chart with 50 hires. At this early stage, that information is more likely to be a distraction than an asset. Your job is to stay focused on the core elements that will make or break your idea in the near term.

I recommend keeping your initial plan to 5-10 pages max. Use bullet points and simple visuals to convey the key points, and push yourself to be concise. The exercise of boiling down your thinking will help you get clearer on what matters most. You can always flesh out additional details later as needed.

Setting clear, achievable goals

In addition to a lean plan, it's important to set some concrete goals for your bootstrapping journey. Having specific, measurable targets will give you a sense of direction, help you prioritize your time and resources, and allow you to celebrate progress along the way.

When I work with bootstrappers, I encourage them to set goals at three levels:

Long-term vision: This is your big, audacious goal - the ultimate impact you want your business to have on the world. It could be something like "Become the go-to solution for [problem] and serve 1 million customers" or "Transform the way people [activity] and build a $100 million company". Your long-term vision should be ambitious enough to inspire you, but not so far-fetched that it feels impossible.

12-month objectives: These are the major milestones you want to hit in the next year. They should be specific, measurable, and directly tied to your long-term vision. For example: "Reach $1 million in annual recurring revenue", "Acquire 10,000 paying customers", or "Expand into 3 new markets". Limit yourself to 3-5 objectives max, so you can stay focused.

90-day initiatives: These are the near-term projects and initiatives that will help you make concrete progress toward your 12-month objectives. They should be actionable, time-bound, and have a clear definition of success. For example: *"Launch version 2.0 of the product with [key features]", "Run a lead generation campaign to acquire 100 new customers"*, or "Hire a head of marketing to own growth initiatives". Again, limit yourself to a handful of initiatives at a time.

The idea is to create a clear line of sight between your day-to-day activities and your ultimate vision. By breaking down your goals into manageable chunks, you can make consistent progress without getting overwhelmed or sidetracked.

As you set your goals, keep in mind the SMART framework: your targets should be Specific, Measurable, Achievable, Relevant, and Time-bound.

Push yourself to be ambitious, but also realistic about what you can accomplish given your resources and stage of growth. It's better to set goals you're reasonably confident you can hit than to aim for the moon and fall short every time.

Remember, your goals are not set in stone. As you gain more information and experience, you'll likely need to adjust your targets. That's totally normal and expected. The key is to have a clear sense of direction and to regularly check in on your progress. I recommend setting aside time each quarter to review your goals, celebrate your wins, and course-correct as needed.

Tools for planning and goal-setting

There are a number of tools and templates you can use to streamline your planning and goal-setting process. Here are a few of my favorites:

Lean Canvas: This is a one-page template for sketching out the key elements of your business model, including your problem, solution, target market, value proposition, and more. It's a great way to quickly iterate on your idea and identify areas of risk or uncertainty.

Business Model Canvas: Similar to the Lean Canvas, this template helps you map out the key components of your business, including your customer segments, revenue streams, key partners, and cost structure. It's a bit more detailed than the Lean Canvas, but still designed to be simple and visual.

OKRs (Objectives and Key Results): This is a popular goal-setting framework used by companies like Google and Intel. The idea is to set high-level objectives, then define the key results that will signify success. For example, an objective might be "Improve customer satisfaction", with key results like "Increase Net Promoter Score from X to Y" and "Reduce support response time by 50%".

SMART goals template: There are many variations of this template available online. Look for one that guides you through defining your goal, specifying how you'll measure success, assessing achievability and relevance, and setting a timeframe.

Project management tools: Once you've set your goals, you'll need a way to track and manage the work required to achieve them. Tools like Trello, Asana, and Notion can help you break down big objectives into smaller tasks, assign owners, and monitor progress.

The specific tools you use are less important than the habit of regular planning and goal-setting. Find a system that works for you and your team, and make it a consistent part of your workflow. By taking the time to get clear on your direction and targets, you'll set yourself up for success as you move into the next phase of your bootstrapping journey.

The importance of flexibility and iteration

Before we wrap up this section on planning and goal-setting, I want to reiterate an important point: your plans will change. No matter how much research and thinking you do upfront, you'll encounter unexpected challenges, opportunities, and insights along the way. The key is to stay flexible and adapt as you learn.

One of the biggest advantages of bootstrapping is that you have the freedom to pivot and iterate quickly based on market feedback. You're not beholden to the expectations of outside investors or the constraints of a rigid plan. If you discover that your initial idea isn't gaining traction, you can make adjustments and try a new approach.

That said, it's important to strike a balance between flexibility and focus. You don't want to be so rigid that you ignore important data, but you also don't want to be so quick to pivot that you never give your ideas a fair shot. Set clear milestones and decision points, and use those to guide your iterations. And when you do make changes to your plan, make sure you're doing it based on real evidence, not just a hunch.

Ultimately, the goal of planning and goal-setting is not to predict the future, but to create a framework for learning and adaptation. By articulating your assumptions, setting clear targets, and regularly checking in on your progress, you'll be well-equipped to navigate the twists and turns of the bootstrapping path.

With a strong foundation in place, you're ready to move on to the next phase of your journey: finding the resources to turn your idea into reality. In the next section, we'll explore a range of funding options for bootstrappers, from personal savings and credit cards to creative alternatives like crowdfunding and revenue-based financing. We'll also discuss how to stretch your limited resources and make smart financial decisions as you grow. Let's dive in.

Chapter 4: Funding Your Business Without VC

One of the biggest challenges of bootstrapping is figuring out how to fund your business without relying on venture capital. While VC can provide a quick influx of cash, it also comes with strings attached - namely, pressure to grow at all costs and loss of control over your company's direction.

As a bootstrapper, you'll need to get creative about how you finance your startup. The good news is that there are more options available today than ever before. In this chapter, we'll explore some of the most common and effective funding strategies for bootstrappers.

Personal savings and credit cards

The simplest and most common way to fund a bootstrapped business is with your own personal savings. This could include money you've set aside specifically for starting a company, as well as funds from a 401k, IRA, or other retirement account (though be sure to consult with a financial advisor before tapping into those).

Using your own money has a few key advantages. First, it allows you to maintain complete control over your business and decision-making. You don't have to answer to anyone else or compromise your vision for the sake of outside investors. Second, it forces you to be disciplined and strategic about how you spend every dollar. When your own hard-earned cash is on the line, you're more likely to make smart, frugal choices.

Of course, funding a startup with personal savings also comes with risks. If the business fails, you could lose a significant chunk of your net worth. That's why it's important to have a solid plan and to only invest money you can afford to lose. Don't put your entire life savings on the line, and make sure you have a backup plan for your personal finances.

In addition to savings, many bootstrappers also rely on credit cards to fund their early expenses. This can be a quick and easy way to access capital, especially if you have good credit and can qualify for cards with

0% introductory APR offers. By spreading expenses across multiple cards and paying off the balances before interest kicks in, you can essentially get a free short-term loan.

However, credit cards are also one of the riskiest ways to fund a startup. If you're unable to pay off your balances right away, you could get stuck with high interest rates and spiraling debt. Credit card debt is notoriously difficult to pay off, and it can put a major strain on your business and personal finances.

If you do decide to use credit cards to fund your startup, be sure to have a plan for paying off your balances quickly. Aim to only charge what you can afford to pay off in a month or two, and avoid maxing out your cards. Use credit as a short-term bridge, not a long-term financing strategy.

Friends and family rounds

Another common funding option for bootstrappers is to raise money from friends and family. This could take the form of a loan, an equity investment, or even just a gift. The advantage of raising money from people you know is that they're often more flexible and patient than outside investors. They may be willing to give you more favorable terms or to wait longer for a return on their investment.

However, mixing business with personal relationships can also be tricky. If things go south with your startup, it could strain or even ruin important friendships and family ties. No one wants to be in a position of losing Grandma's retirement savings or having an awkward Thanksgiving dinner with a resentful uncle.

If you do decide to raise money from friends and family, be sure to treat it like a professional business transaction. Put everything in writing, including the terms of the investment, repayment schedule, and what happens if the business fails. Make it clear that investing in a startup is risky, and don't pressure anyone to contribute more than they can afford to lose.

It's also a good idea to set clear boundaries and expectations around communication and involvement. Just because someone invests in your company doesn't mean they get to weigh in on every decision or drop by the office unannounced. Establish professional norms early on to avoid conflicts down the road.

Crowdfunding

In recent years, crowdfunding has emerged as a popular way for bootstrappers to raise money and validate demand for their products. Platforms like Kickstarter and Indiegogo allow entrepreneurs to campaign for funding from the public, typically in exchange for pre-orders, discounts, or other rewards.

The beauty of crowdfunding is that it lets you test the market and build buzz around your offering before you've built anything. If people are willing to put down money for your product before it even exists, that's a strong signal that you're onto something. A successful crowdfunding campaign can also help you attract press coverage, grow your email list, and gather valuable feedback from early adopters.

Of course, running a successful crowdfunding campaign is no easy feat. It requires significant preparation, marketing hustle, and follow-through. You'll need to put together a compelling video and pitch, come up with enticing rewards, and promote your campaign aggressively through your network and beyond. And once the campaign ends, you'll need to buckle down and actually deliver on your promises to backers.

Crowdfunding is best-suited for consumer products, creative projects, and other offerings that lend themselves to a pre-order model. It's less common for B2B or SaaS startups, though there are always exceptions. If you do go the crowdfunding route, be sure to study successful campaigns in your category and aim to replicate their strategies.

Grants and pitch competitions

Another potential funding source for bootstrappers is grants and pitch competitions. Depending on your industry and location, you may be eligible for government grants, foundation awards, or other non-dilutive funding. These programs are often targeted at specific types of businesses, such as those led by women or minorities, those focused on social or environmental impact, or those operating in certain sectors like biotech or clean energy.

To find grant opportunities, start by searching online databases like **Grants.gov and GrantWatch.** You can also reach out to your local Small Business Development Center, Chamber of Commerce, or industry association for leads. Be prepared to put together detailed applications and proposals that make a compelling case for your business.

Pitch competitions are another way to potentially secure grant funding, as well as exposure and mentorship. These events typically involve entrepreneurs presenting their business ideas to a panel of judges, with the winners receiving cash prizes and other support. Well-known programs include TechCrunch Disrupt, MassChallenge, and the Rice Business Plan Competition.

To succeed in a pitch competition, you'll need to hone your storytelling skills and create a concise, compelling presentation. Practice your pitch in front of different audiences and incorporate their feedback. Be sure to highlight your unique value proposition, market opportunity, and traction to date. And don't forget to close with a clear ask - how much money you're seeking and what you plan to use it for.

While grants and pitch competitions can provide valuable infusions of cash, they're also highly competitive and time-consuming to pursue. Don't bank your entire funding strategy on winning a long-shot award. Instead, view these opportunities as a supplementary source of capital that can help you stretch your runway and build credibility.

Customer funding and pre-sales

Perhaps the most appealing way to fund a bootstrapped business is with money from actual customers. After all, if people are willing to pay for your product or service, that's the ultimate validation of your idea. There are a few different ways to tap into customer funding:

Pre-sales: This involves selling your product before you've actually built it, often at a discount. This can be a good way to gauge demand, generate cash flow, and fund production. However, it also comes with risks - if you're unable to deliver on your promises, you could end up with angry customers and damaged credibility. Only pursue pre-sales if you're confident in your ability to follow through.

Subscriptions and recurring revenue: If you have a product or service that lends itself to a recurring model, you can fund your business with predictable, ongoing revenue from subscribers. This is a common approach for SaaS, content, and other types of businesses with low marginal costs. By signing up customers for monthly or annual plans, you can smooth out your cash flow and reinvest profits into growth.

Selling services: Another way to generate customer revenue is by selling services related to your core offering. For example, if you're building a software product, you could offer consulting, training, or custom development to early clients. This can be a good way to bring in cash while also gathering valuable feedback and use cases. Just be careful not to get too distracted from your main focus.

Whichever approach you choose, the key is to start generating revenue as early as possible. Don't wait until your product is perfect to start selling. Look for ways to create value for customers from day one, even if it's in a limited or MVP form. The sooner you can get money coming in the door, the more runway you'll have to iterate and grow.

Bootstrapper-friendly loans and financing

While taking on debt is often seen as anathema to bootstrapping, there are some forms of financing that can be compatible with a self-funded approach. The key is to look for loans and credit lines with favorable terms and repayment structures.

SBA microloans: The U.S. Small Business Administration offers microloans of up to $50,000 to help small businesses start up and expand. These loans are administered through nonprofit community lenders and typically have more flexible eligibility requirements than traditional bank loans. Interest rates are generally between 8-13%, with repayment terms of up to six years.

Revenue-based financing: This newer form of funding allows businesses to borrow against their future revenue, rather than giving up equity or collateral. Lenders provide cash upfront in exchange for a percentage of the company's monthly revenue until the loan is repaid, plus a flat fee. This can be a good option for companies with predictable revenue streams and healthy margins.

Equipment financing: If your business requires expensive equipment or machinery, you may be able to finance those purchases through equipment loans or leases. These often come with lower interest rates and longer repayment terms than traditional loans, since the equipment itself serves as collateral. Just be sure to crunch the numbers and make sure the monthly payments fit your cash flow projections.

Invoice factoring: For businesses that invoice customers and have to wait to get paid, invoice factoring can provide a short-term cash infusion.

With factoring, you sell your outstanding invoices to a third party at a discount, and they give you a lump sum of cash upfront. When your customers pay their invoices, the money goes to the factoring company. This can be a good way to smooth out lumpy cash flow, but be aware that factoring fees can add up.

Before taking on any kind of debt, be sure to shop around for the best rates and terms. Look for lenders that specialize in working with startups and have experience in your industry. Read the fine print carefully and make sure you understand all the fees, covenants, and repayment obligations. And above all, borrow conscientiously - only take on debt you're confident you can repay, and use it for investments that will generate a positive return.

Parting thoughts

Funding a bootstrapped business is not for the faint of heart. It requires creativity, discipline, and a willingness to hustle like crazy. But for entrepreneurs who value control and self-sufficiency, bootstrapping can be an incredibly rewarding path.

The key is to stay scrappy and make the most of the resources you do have. Focus on generating revenue early and often. Be relentless about controlling costs and extending your runway. And don't be afraid to get creative with your funding strategies - whether that means bartering services, launching a crowdfunding campaign, or even selling your car.

Remember, the goal of bootstrapping is not to avoid outside capital forever, but to get to a point where you can dictate the terms. By building a lean, profitable business from the ground up, you'll be in a much stronger position when it comes time to raise money or exit on your own terms. So embrace the challenge and get ready to bootstrap your way to success.

Chapter 5: Building a Minimum Viable Product (MVP) with Limited Resources

As a bootstrapper, one of your most critical tasks is to validate your business idea as quickly and cheaply as possible. You don't have the luxury of spending months or years perfecting your product in a vacuum - you need to get it into the hands of real customers and start gathering feedback ASAP.

This is where the concept of a Minimum Viable Product (MVP) comes in. An MVP is the most basic version of your product that allows you to test your core hypothesis with minimal investment. It's not meant to be perfect or feature-complete - it's simply a way to gauge whether people are interested in what you're offering and willing to pay for it.

The beauty of an MVP is that it forces you to focus on the most essential aspects of your product and ruthlessly cut everything else. By stripping away bells and whistles, you can build something quickly and get it to market faster. This not only saves you time and money, but it also allows you to start learning from real customer behavior and iterate accordingly.

Of course, building an MVP on a bootstrapper's budget is easier said than done. You'll need to get creative with your resources and make smart trade-offs along the way. In this chapter, we'll explore some strategies for developing a lean, effective MVP that sets you up for success.

Define your core value proposition

Before you start building anything, you need to get crystal clear on what problem you're solving and for whom. What is the unique value that your product delivers to customers? How does it make their lives better or easier in a meaningful way?

Start by talking to potential customers and deeply understanding their needs, pain points, and desires. Look for patterns and insights that can help you hone in on the most critical aspects of your offering. What features or benefits come up again and again? What gets people excited or motivated to take action?

Once you have a handle on your core value prop, distill it down to a simple, concise statement that captures the essence of what you're offering. This will serve as your north star as you make decisions about what to include in your MVP and what to leave out.

For example, when Dropbox was first getting started, its core value prop was dead simple: "Sync your files online and across your computers." This laser focus on a single, high-value feature allowed the company to build a lean MVP that resonated with early adopters and set the stage for future growth.

Identify your riskiest assumptions

Every business idea rests on a set of assumptions about the market, the customer, and the product itself. Some of these assumptions are riskier than others - meaning if they turn out to be wrong, they could sink your entire venture.

As you're planning your MVP, it's crucial to identify your riskiest assumptions and design experiments to test them. These could include things like:

- Will customers actually pay for this product or service?
- Can we acquire customers at a sustainable cost?
- Will people use the product as intended and get value from it?
- Can we deliver the product or service at a profitable price point?

By tackling these big, hairy questions early on, you can avoid wasting time and money on a flawed concept. You might discover that you need to pivot your approach or even scrap the idea altogether - but better to find that out sooner rather than later.

To test your assumptions, look for ways to create lightweight, low-cost experiments that give you real-world data. This could involve things like:

Landing page tests: Create a simple website that describes your product or service and asks people to sign up for more information. Track how many people visit the page and convert to get a sense of overall interest.

Pre-sales: Offer your product for sale before it's actually built, either through a crowdfunding campaign or by taking pre-orders on your website. If people are willing to put down money sight unseen, that's a strong signal of demand.

Concierge MVP: Manually provide the core value of your product to a small group of customers, even if it's not scalable. For example, if you're building a meal delivery service, you could start by cooking and delivering the meals yourself to test out the concept.

Wizard of Oz MVP: Create the illusion of a fully functional product, but manually handle tasks behind the scenes. For instance, if you're building an AI-powered chatbot, you could start by having a human respond to user inquiries in real-time while you're developing the actual technology.

The key is to start with the simplest, fastest experiment that will give you the information you need to make a decision. Don't get caught up in building a perfect prototype or gathering exhaustive data. The goal is to learn quickly and iterate based on feedback.

Prioritize features ruthlessly

Once you've defined your core value prop and identified your riskiest assumptions, it's time to start actually designing and building your MVP. This is where the rubber meets the road in terms of making tough trade-offs and prioritizing what's truly essential.

One helpful framework for feature prioritization is the MoSCoW method:

Must-haves: These are the core features that are absolutely essential for delivering your value prop and testing your key assumptions. Without these, you don't really have a viable product.

Should-haves: These are important features that add significant value, but aren't strictly necessary for launching a bare-bones version. You should include these if time and resources allow.

Could-haves: These are nice-to-have features that would be great to include, but can easily be left out of the initial release. Think of these as potential enhancements for future iterations.

Won't-haves: These are features that are explicitly excluded from the current scope, either because they're not relevant to the core value prop or because they're too complex to include in the MVP.

As you're categorizing features, be brutally honest about what truly moves the needle for your customers. Don't get sidetracked by "vanity metrics" or surface-level improvements that don't address the core problem. And be willing to cut even good ideas if they're not absolutely critical for getting to market quickly.

For example, when Twitter first launched, its MVP was essentially just a single feature: the ability to post short status updates (called "tweets") via SMS. There were no @replies, no hashtags, no retweets or likes. Just a simple way to share what you were doing with your friends in real-time. By focusing on this core use case, Twitter was able to get to market quickly and start learning from real user behavior.

Of course, as you're prioritizing features, it's important to keep in mind the technical feasibility and resource requirements of each one. There's no point in including a "must-have" feature in your MVP if it's going to take months to build and blow your budget. Be realistic about what you can accomplish with the time, money, and skills you have available.

Leverage existing tools and platforms

One of the biggest mistakes bootstrappers make when building an MVP is trying to reinvent the wheel at every turn. They assume they need to build everything from scratch, which can lead to ballooning costs and endless delays. In reality, there are a wealth of existing tools and platforms you can leverage to get your MVP off the ground quickly and cheaply.

For example, let's say you're building a mobile app for ordering custom t-shirts. Rather than spending months and thousands of dollars developing your own e-commerce backend and design tools, you could:

- Use a platform like Shopify or BigCommerce to handle payments, order processing, and inventory management.
- Integrate with a print-on-demand service like Printful or Teelaunch to handle production and fulfillment.
- Use a drag-and-drop design tool like Canva or Placeit to let customers create their own t-shirt designs.

By stitching together these existing components, you could have a functional MVP up and running in a matter of weeks, with minimal custom development required.

The same principle applies to almost any type of digital product or service. Need a way for users to book appointments? Use a tool like Calendly or Acuity. Want to let customers chat with each other in real-time? Integrate a service like Pusher or Firebase. Need to process payments? Use Stripe or PayPal.

Of course, there will likely be some custom development required to tie everything together and create a seamless user experience. But by leveraging existing tools and platforms wherever possible, you can dramatically reduce the time and cost of getting your MVP to market.

Prioritize speed over perfection

When you're bootstrapping an MVP, it's easy to get caught up in the quest for perfection. You want every pixel to be polished, every edge case to be accounted for, every potential flaw to be ironed out before you launch. But the reality is, perfection is the enemy of progress. The longer you wait to get your product in front of real users, the more time and money you'll waste on things that may not even matter.

The key is to prioritize speed over perfection. Focus on getting a functional, usable version of your product out the door as quickly as possible, even if it's a little rough around the edges. As LinkedIn founder Reid Hoffman famously said, "If you're not embarrassed by the first version of your product, you've launched too late."

This doesn't mean you should ship shoddy or buggy software. But it does mean being willing to make trade-offs and cut corners in the name of getting to market faster. For example:

- Instead of building a fully-featured onboarding flow, start with a simple welcome email and a link to your documentation.
- Rather than investing in pixel-perfect design, use a pre-built UI kit or template to get up and running quickly.
- Instead of trying to automate every process from day one, start with manual workarounds and gradually automate as you scale.

The goal is to get something – anything – in the hands of real users as soon as possible. Once you're out in the wild, you can start gathering feedback, iterating on your design, and gradually improving the user experience over time.

Of course, there are some areas where you can't afford to cut corners. Security, privacy, and data integrity should always be top priorities, even in an

MVP. And if you're building hardware or physical products, you'll need to be extra diligent about testing and quality control. But in general, the faster you can get your product to market, the faster you can start learning and improving.

Measure and iterate

Building an MVP is just the beginning of your journey as a bootstrapper. Once you've launched your product, the real work begins in terms of measuring your success, gathering feedback, and iterating on your design.

To start, make sure you have clear, measurable goals for your MVP. What metrics will you use to gauge traction and user engagement? How will you know if your product is resonating with your target audience? Some key things to track might include:

- **Acquisition:** How many people are signing up for your product or service? Where are they coming from? What channels are most effective for reaching your target customers?

- **Activation:** How many users are actually using your product after signing up? What percentage are completing key onboarding steps or reaching critical milestones?
- **Retention:** How many users are sticking around over time? What's your churn rate? What factors are contributing to user retention or attrition?
- **Revenue:** If you're charging for your product, how much money are you making? What's your average revenue per user? What's your customer lifetime value?
- **Referral:** Are your users recommending your product to others? What's your viral coefficient? How can you encourage more word-of-mouth growth?

By tracking these metrics closely, you can start to get a sense of what's working and what's not. You can identify areas for improvement and start making data-driven decisions about where to invest your limited resources.

Of course, metrics only tell part of the story. To really understand how users are experiencing your product, you need to talk to them directly. Conduct user interviews, send out surveys, and gather qualitative feedback whenever possible. Ask open-ended questions like:

- What do you like most about our product? What do you find frustrating or confusing?
- How does our product compare to other solutions you've tried? What made you switch?
- What additional features or functionality would make our product more valuable to you?
- What would make you recommend our product to others?

By combining quantitative data with qualitative insights, you can start to paint a more complete picture of your product's strengths and weaknesses.

As you gather feedback and identify areas for improvement, it's important to prioritize your efforts based on impact and feasibility. Focus on the changes that will have the biggest positive impact on your key metrics, while also being realistic about what you can accomplish with your limited resources.

And remember, iteration is a continuous process. Your MVP is just the starting point – you should always be looking for ways to refine and improve your product based on user feedback and changing market conditions. The most successful bootstrappers are the ones who are constantly learning, adapting, and evolving their offerings to better serve their customers.

Final Thought on Building MVP

Building an MVP on a bootstrapper's budget is no easy feat. It requires focus, discipline, and a willingness to make tough trade-offs in the name of getting to market quickly. But by following the strategies outlined in this chapter – defining your core value prop, identifying your riskiest assumptions, prioritizing features ruthlessly, leveraging existing tools, and focusing on speed over perfection – you can greatly increase your chances of success.

Remember, your MVP is just the first step in a long journey of iteration and improvement. The real magic happens when you start gathering feedback from real users and using that data to inform your product roadmap. By staying focused on your customers' needs and continuously refining your offering, you can build a product that people love and a business that stands the test of time.

So don't be afraid to get started, even if your MVP is a little rough around the edges. The most important thing is to get something out there and start learning. With a bit of grit, creativity, and perseverance, you can bootstrap your way to a successful product – one that delivers real value to your customers and sets you up for long-term growth.

Chapter 6: Marketing on a Budget: Grassroots Strategies, Social Media, and Networking

As a bootstrapper, you can't afford to spend big bucks on flashy marketing campaigns or expensive ad placements. Every dollar counts when you're self-funding your business, so you need to be strategic and scrappy in your approach to customer acquisition.

The good news is, there are plenty of low-cost and even free ways to get the word out about your product and start building a loyal customer base. In this chapter, we'll explore some proven grassroots marketing strategies that any bootstrapper can use to generate buzz, drive traffic, and close sales on a shoestring budget.

Leverage your personal network

One of the most powerful marketing assets you have as a bootstrapper is your personal network. The people who know you, like you, and trust you can be invaluable allies in spreading the word about your product and helping you land your first customers.

Start by making a list of everyone in your personal and professional network who might be interested in what you're building. This could include:

- Friends and family members
- Former colleagues and classmates
- Industry contacts and thought leaders
- Social media followers and online communities

Once you have your list, reach out to each person individually and let them know about your new venture. But don't just ask for their help – offer something of value in return. This could be an exclusive discount, early access to your product, or even just a heartfelt thank you.

The key is to make your outreach personal and authentic. Don't blast out a generic email or social media post – take the time to craft a thoughtful message that speaks directly to each person's interests and needs. And be sure to follow up and stay in touch over time – building strong relationships is key to turning your network into a powerful marketing engine.

Tap into online communities

Another great way to get the word out about your product is to tap into online communities where your target customers congregate. These could be forums, social media groups, Reddit threads, or even email newsletters and blogs.

Start by identifying the communities that are most relevant to your product or industry. Look for groups with high engagement and a strong sense of community – places where people are actively sharing ideas, asking questions, and helping each other out.

Once you've found a few promising communities, take some time to observe the conversation and get a feel for the group's culture and norms. Don't just jump in and start promoting your product right away – that's a surefire way to turn people off and get kicked out of the group.

Instead, focus on adding value to the conversation. Share your expertise, answer questions, and offer helpful resources and insights. As you build trust and credibility within the community, you can start to mention your product in a natural, non-promotional way.

For example, let's say you've built a new project management tool for remote teams. You might start by joining a few online communities for remote workers and digital nomads. You could share your own experiences working remotely, offer tips and best practices for staying productive, and even create a few free resources like templates or checklists.

As you become known as a helpful and knowledgeable member of the community, you can start to casually mention your product as a tool that's helped you and your team work more efficiently. You might even offer a special discount or free trial to community members who are interested in trying it out.

The key is to focus on building genuine relationships and adding value, rather than just trying to make a quick sale. By establishing yourself as a trusted expert and partner, you'll be much more likely to attract loyal customers who will spread the word about your product to their own networks.

Create valuable content

When we talk of digital domination today regarding online marketing, content is king. By creating valuable, informative, and engaging content that speaks directly to your target audience's needs and interests, you can attract potential customers, build trust and credibility, and even generate organic search traffic over time.

The type of content you create will depend on your product, industry, and target audience. Some common formats include:

- Blog posts and articles
- Videos and webinars
- Podcasts and interviews
- Infographics and visual content
- Ebooks and whitepapers

- Case studies and customer stories

The key is to focus on creating content that is genuinely helpful and valuable to your target audience. Don't just churn out self-promotional fluff – take the time to understand your customers' pain points, challenges, and goals, and create content that speaks directly to those needs.

For example, let's say you've created a new app that helps people stick to their fitness routines. You might create content like:

- A blog post on "10 Ways to Stay Motivated When You Don't Feel Like Working Out"
- A video tutorial on how to use your app to create a personalized workout plan
- An infographic on the benefits of regular exercise for mental and physical health
- A case study featuring a customer who lost 50 pounds using your app

By creating content that is both informative and engaging, you can attract potential customers who are actively searching for solutions to their problems. And by optimizing your content for search engines and promoting it through social media and other channels, you can drive traffic back to your website and start building a loyal audience over time.

Of course, creating high-quality content takes time and effort – two things that are often in short supply for bootstrappers. That's why it's important to be strategic about the types of content you create and the channels you use to promote it.

Start by focusing on a few key topics or themes that are closely related to your product and target audience. Create a content calendar to help you plan out your posts and ensure a consistent publishing schedule. And don't be afraid to repurpose your content across multiple formats and channels – a single blog post could be turned into a video, a podcast episode, and a series of social media posts.

Leverage social media

Social media is another powerful tool for bootstrappers looking to market their products on a budget. By building a strong presence on platforms like Twitter, Facebook, Instagram, and LinkedIn, you can connect with potential customers, build brand awareness, and even drive direct sales.

The key to success on social media is to focus on engagement and value, rather than just promotion. Don't just blast out self-serving sales pitches – take the time to listen to your followers, respond to their comments and questions, and share content that is genuinely interesting and useful to them.

Some tips for maximizing your social media marketing efforts:

- **Choose the right platforms:** Not all social media platforms are created equal. Focus your efforts on the ones where your target audience is most active and engaged.

- **Optimize your profiles:** Make sure your social media profiles are complete, up-to-date, and on-brand. Use high-quality images, compelling descriptions, and relevant keywords to make it easy for people to find and connect with you.
- **Share a mix of content:** In addition to promoting your own products and content, share relevant industry news, helpful resources, and engaging visual content like images and videos.
- **Engage with your followers:** Respond to comments and messages in a timely and helpful way. Ask questions, run polls and surveys, and encourage your followers to share their own experiences and feedback.
- **Use hashtags strategically:** Hashtags can help your content reach a wider audience and attract new followers. Use relevant, popular hashtags that are specific to your industry or niche.
- **Run contests and giveaways:** Offering prizes and incentives can be a great way to generate buzz and attract new followers. Just be sure to follow each platform's rules and guidelines for promotions.

By building a strong social media presence and engaging with your followers on a regular basis, you can create a community of loyal fans and advocates who will help spread the word about your product and drive organic growth over time.

Partner with influencers and thought leaders

Another way to get your product in front of a wider audience is to partner with influencers and thought leaders in your industry. These are people who have already built a large and engaged following, and whose endorsement can carry a lot of weight with potential customers.

Of course, as a bootstrapper, you may not have the budget to pay for high-profile influencer campaigns. But that doesn't mean you can't still leverage the power of influencer marketing in a more grassroots way.

Start by identifying influencers and thought leaders who are a good fit for your product and audience. Look for people who have a genuine interest in your industry or niche, and whose values and approach align with your own.

Then, reach out to them directly and introduce yourself and your product. But don't just ask for their endorsement right away – focus on building a relationship first. Offer to collaborate on content, share their work with your own audience, or even just send them a free sample of your product to try out.

As you build trust and rapport with these influencers, you can start to explore more formal partnership opportunities. This could include:

Guest blogging or podcast appearances

- Joint webinars or live events
- Product reviews or sponsored content
- Affiliate marketing or revenue-sharing arrangements

The key is to approach these partnerships as a two-way street. Don't just focus on what the influencer can do for you – think about how you can add value to their audience and help them achieve their own goals as well.

By partnering with respected influencers and thought leaders in your industry, you can tap into their audience and credibility to drive awareness and sales for your own product. Just be sure to choose your partners carefully and focus on building genuine, mutually beneficial relationships over time.

Get creative with guerrilla marketing

Finally, don't be afraid to get creative with your marketing efforts and think outside the box. Guerrilla marketing is all about using unconventional, low-cost tactics to generate buzz and awareness for your brand.

Some examples of guerrilla marketing tactics that bootstrappers can use:

- **Sticker or poster campaigns:** Create eye-catching stickers or posters featuring your brand and product, and distribute them in

high-traffic areas like coffee shops, co-working spaces, or college campuses.
- **Flash mobs or street performances:** Organize a surprise event or performance in a public space, and use it to promote your product or brand in a fun and engaging way.
- **Scavenger hunts or treasure hunts:** Create a game or challenge that encourages people to engage with your brand and product, and offer prizes or incentives for participation.
- **Viral videos or stunts:** Create a funny, surprising, or thought-provoking video or stunt that has the potential to go viral on social media and generate buzz for your brand.
- **Guerrilla sampling:** Get creative with product sampling by handing out free samples in unexpected places or ways, like attaching them to bike handlebars or leaving them in public park benches.

The key to successful guerrilla marketing is to be creative, bold, and memorable. Look for opportunities to surprise and delight your target audience, and create experiences that they'll want to share with their friends and followers.

Of course, guerrilla marketing can also be risky if not done carefully. Always make sure to follow local laws and regulations, and avoid tactics that could be seen as spammy, intrusive, or offensive. Focus on creating genuine value and engagement, rather than just trying to shock or provoke for the sake of attention.

Measure and optimize your efforts

No matter which marketing strategies you choose to pursue, it's important to track your results and continually optimize your efforts over time. This means setting clear goals and KPIs for each tactic, and using data and analytics to measure your progress and identify areas for improvement.

Some key metrics to track might include:

- **Website traffic and engagement:** Use tools like Google Analytics to track how many people are visiting your website, where they're coming from, and how they're engaging with your content and product pages.

- **Social media metrics:** Track your follower growth, engagement rates, and click-through rates on each social media platform to see which types of content and tactics are resonating with your audience.
- **Email marketing metrics:** Monitor your email open rates, click-through rates, and conversion rates to see how effective your email campaigns are at driving engagement and sales.
- **Sales and revenue:** Of course, the ultimate measure of success for any marketing effort is whether it's driving actual business results. Track your sales and revenue numbers closely, and look for correlations between specific marketing tactics and spikes in sales or customer acquisition.

By regularly tracking and analyzing your marketing metrics, you can identify what's working well and what's not, and make data-driven decisions about where to focus your efforts and resources going forward.

It's also important to remember that marketing is an ongoing process, not a one-time event. Even if you have a successful product launch or campaign, you can't just sit back and rest on your laurels. Keep experimenting with new tactics and strategies, and always be looking for ways to improve and optimize your marketing efforts over time.

Final Thought on Marketing on a Budget

Marketing on a bootstrapper's budget can be challenging, but it's far from impossible. By leveraging your personal network, tapping into online communities, creating valuable content, using social media strategically, partnering with influencers, and getting creative with guerrilla marketing tactics, you can build buzz and drive sales for your product without breaking the bank.

The key is to focus on building genuine relationships and adding value to your target audience, rather than just trying to sell them something. By establishing yourself as a trusted expert and partner, and creating experiences that people will want to share and talk about, you can attract loyal customers and advocates who will help spread the word about your product and fuel your growth over time.

Of course, marketing is just one piece of the puzzle when it comes to bootstrapping a successful business. In the next chapter, we'll explore some strategies for generating revenue early on, even before your product is fully developed or launched. By starting to bring in cash flow from day one, you can extend your runway, validate your business model, and set yourself up for long-term success as a bootstrapped founder.

Chapter 7: Generating Revenue Early: Pre-Sales, Subscriptions, and Multiple Revenue Streams

One of the biggest challenges of bootstrapping a business is managing your cash flow. Without the safety net of venture capital, you need to be laser-focused on generating revenue as quickly as possible to keep your business afloat and fund your growth.

The good news is, there are plenty of ways to start bringing in money even before your product is fully developed or launched. By getting creative with your revenue model and offering value to customers in innovative ways, you can start generating cash flow from day one and give yourself the runway you need to scale your business over time.

In this chapter, we'll explore some proven strategies for generating revenue early on, including pre-sales, subscriptions, and multiple revenue streams. We'll also discuss how to price your product effectively and build a sustainable business model that can support your long-term growth and success.

Pre-sell your product before it's built

One of the most effective ways to generate revenue early on is to pre-sell your product before it's even built. This means offering customers the chance to buy your product at a discounted rate in exchange for paying upfront and waiting for delivery at a later date.

Pre-selling can be a powerful way to validate demand for your product, generate cash flow to fund development, and build buzz and anticipation among your target audience. It can also help you gauge interest in different features or pricing models, and get valuable feedback from early adopters that can inform your product roadmap.

To run a successful pre-sale campaign, you'll need to create a compelling offer that incentivizes customers to buy now rather than wait for your product to be fully launched. This could include:

- **Early bird discounts:** Offer a significant discount (e.g. 50% off) to customers who pre-order your product before a certain date.
- **Exclusive bonuses:** Include additional features, content, or services for customers who pre-order, such as a private community forum or one-on-one coaching sessions.
- **Limited edition products:** Create a special version of your product that's only available to pre-order customers, such as a signed copy of your book or a custom-designed t-shirt.
- **Tiered pricing:** Offer different price points based on when customers pre-order, with the lowest prices available to the earliest buyers.

Once you've created your pre-sale offer, you'll need to promote it heavily to your target audience through email marketing, social media, and other channels. Make sure to clearly communicate the benefits of pre-ordering, as well as the timeline for when customers can expect to receive their product.

It's also important to be transparent about the status of your product development and any potential delays or changes in scope. Keep customers updated regularly on your progress, and be proactive in addressing any concerns or questions they may have.

By running a successful pre-sale campaign, you can generate significant revenue before your product is even finished, and build a loyal base of early adopters who are invested in your success.

Offer a subscription or recurring revenue model

Another way to generate predictable, ongoing revenue is to offer your product or service on a subscription or recurring basis. This means charging customers a fixed fee on a monthly, quarterly, or annual basis in exchange for access to your product or service over time.

Subscription-based models can be particularly effective for businesses that offer software, content, or other digital products that customers need on an ongoing basis. By providing a steady stream of value over time, you can create a loyal customer base that is less likely to churn and more likely to refer others to your business.

To create a successful subscription model, you'll need to carefully consider your pricing strategy and the value you're providing to customers. Some key factors to consider include:

- **Frequency of billing:** Will you charge customers monthly, quarterly, or annually? Monthly billing can be more attractive to customers who are hesitant to commit to a long-term contract, but annual billing can provide more predictable revenue and reduce churn.
- **Pricing tiers:** Will you offer different pricing tiers based on features, usage, or other factors? Tiered pricing can help you attract a wider range of customers and upsell them over time as their needs grow.
- **Free trials or freemium models:** Will you offer a free trial or a limited version of your product for free, with the goal of converting users to paid subscribers over time? Freemium models can be effective for attracting a large user base quickly, but you'll need to carefully balance the costs of supporting free users with the revenue generated by paid subscribers.

- **Retention and churn:** How will you keep subscribers engaged and minimize churn over time? This could include offering regular updates and new features, providing excellent customer support, and creating a sense of community and belonging among your users.

By creating a subscription model that provides ongoing value to customers and generates predictable revenue for your business, you can create a more sustainable and scalable business model that can support your growth over time.

Develop multiple revenue streams

Another way to generate more predictable and diversified revenue is to develop multiple streams of income for your business. This means offering a range of products or services that appeal to different segments of your target audience and generate revenue in different ways.

For example, let's say you're building a software product that helps small businesses manage their social media marketing. In addition to offering your core product on a subscription basis, you could also:

- Offer one-on-one coaching or consulting services to help businesses develop and execute their social media strategy.
- Create and sell online courses or workshops on social media marketing best practices.
- Develop a marketplace for social media templates, graphics, and other resources that businesses can purchase and use in their marketing campaigns.
- Partner with other businesses to offer bundle deals or cross-promotions to your shared target audience.

By diversifying your revenue streams, you can create a more resilient and adaptable business model that can withstand changes in the market or shifts in customer behavior. You can also create more value for your customers by offering a range of products and services that meet their evolving needs over time.

Of course, developing multiple revenue streams can also be more complex and time-consuming than focusing on a single core product. You'll need to carefully consider the resources and skills required to develop and support each new offering, as well as the potential impact on your brand and customer experience.

To create successful multiple revenue streams, it's important to:

- **Focus on your core strengths:** Look for opportunities to leverage your existing skills, knowledge, and resources to create new products or services that complement your core offering.
- **Listen to your customers:** Pay attention to the needs and pain points of your target audience, and look for ways to create new offerings that address those needs in a unique and valuable way.
- **Test and iterate:** Don't be afraid to experiment with new ideas and revenue models, but be sure to track your results and iterate based on customer feedback and data.

- **Communicate clearly:** Make sure your customers understand the full range of products and services you offer, and how they can benefit from each one. Use clear and consistent messaging across all your marketing and sales channels.

By developing multiple revenue streams that align with your core strengths and meet the evolving needs of your target audience, you can create a more sustainable and profitable business model that can support your growth over the long term.

Price your product effectively

Of course, generating revenue is not just about offering the right products or services – it's also about pricing them effectively. The price you charge for your product or service can have a significant impact on your revenue, profitability, and overall business success.

When setting your prices, there are a few key factors to consider:

- **Cost of goods sold (COGS):** This includes the direct costs of producing and delivering your product or service, such as materials, labor, and shipping. Make sure your prices are high enough to cover your COGS and still leave room for a healthy profit margin.
- **Market demand:** Consider the overall demand for your product or service in the market, as well as the willingness of your target customers to pay for it. If demand is high and your product is unique or valuable, you may be able to charge a premium price. If demand is lower or there are many competitors in your market, you may need to price more aggressively to attract customers.
- **Perceived value:** The perceived value of your product or service can also impact how much customers are willing to pay for it. If your product is seen as high-quality, innovative, or exclusive, you may be able to charge a higher price than if it's seen as a commodity or a basic necessity.
- **Pricing strategy:** There are several common pricing strategies you can use, depending on your business model and goals. These include:

- **Cost-plus pricing:** This involves adding a fixed markup to your COGS to determine your price. This can be a simple and straightforward approach, but it may not always align with market demand or perceived value.
- **Value-based pricing:** This involves setting your prices based on the perceived value of your product or service to your target customers. This can allow you to charge a premium price for high-value offerings, but it requires a deep understanding of your customers and their needs.
- **Competitive pricing:** This involves setting your prices based on what your competitors are charging for similar products or services. This can help you stay competitive in your market, but it may not always reflect the true value of your offering.
- **Penetration pricing:** This involves setting a low initial price to attract customers and gain market share quickly, with the goal of raising prices over time as you build brand loyalty and recognition.

Ultimately, the right pricing strategy for your business will depend on your specific goals, target audience, and competitive landscape. It may take some experimentation and iteration to find the sweet spot that maximizes your revenue and profitability while still providing value to your customers.

As you set your prices and develop your revenue model, it's also important to keep in mind the long-term sustainability and scalability of your business. Make sure your prices are high enough to cover your costs and generate a healthy profit margin, but not so high that they turn off potential customers or limit your ability to grow.

Test and adapt over time

Finally, it's important to remember that generating revenue is an ongoing process that requires continuous testing, learning, and adaptation. As you launch new products or services, experiment with different pricing models, and seek to diversify your revenue streams, be sure to track your results and gather feedback from your customers along the way.

Some key metrics to track include:

- **Revenue**: How much total revenue are you generating from each product or service, and how does this compare to your goals and projections?
- **Customer acquisition costs (CAC):** How much does it cost you to acquire each new customer, and how does this compare to the lifetime value (LTV) of those customers?
- **Churn rate:** How many customers are leaving your business each month or year, and why? High churn rates can be a sign that your product or pricing model is not meeting the needs of your target audience.
- **Net promoter score (NPS):** This is a measure of how likely your customers are to recommend your business to others. A high NPS can be a sign of strong customer loyalty and satisfaction.

By regularly tracking and analyzing these metrics, you can identify areas for improvement and make data-driven decisions about how to optimize your revenue model over time. This may involve adjusting your prices, adding or removing products or services, or experimenting with new marketing or sales strategies.

Remember, generating revenue is not a one-time event — it's an ongoing process that requires continuous effort and adaptation. By staying focused on your customers, leveraging your strengths, and being willing to experiment and iterate, you can build a sustainable and profitable business model that can support your long-term growth and success.

Final Thought

Generating revenue early and often is critical for bootstrapped businesses that don't have the luxury of venture capital to fall back on. By getting creative with your revenue model and offering value to customers in innovative ways, you can start bringing in cash flow from day one and give yourself the runway you need to scale your business over time.

Whether you choose to pre-sell your product, offer a subscription model, develop multiple revenue streams, or experiment with different pricing strategies, the key is to stay focused on your customers and their evolving needs. By continuously testing, learning, and adapting your approach based on data and feedback, you can build a sustainable and profitable business that can weather the ups and downs of the entrepreneurial journey.

In the next chapter, we'll explore some strategies for operating lean and keeping your costs low as you scale your business over time. From outsourcing non-core functions to managing your cash flow effectively, we'll discuss how to maximize your resources and minimize your risk as you grow and evolve your bootstrapped business.

Chapter 8: Operating Lean: Keeping Costs Low, Outsourcing, and Managing Cash Flow

As a bootstrapped founder, one of your biggest priorities is to keep your costs as low as possible while still delivering value to your customers and growing your business. This means being strategic about how you allocate your limited resources, and finding ways to maximize your output while minimizing your expenses.

In this chapter, we'll explore some key strategies for operating lean as you scale your bootstrapped business over time. From outsourcing non-core functions to managing your cash flow effectively, we'll discuss how to stay nimble and efficient as you navigate the challenges of growth and expansion.

Keep your fixed costs low

One of the most important ways to operate lean is to keep your fixed costs as low as possible. Fixed costs are expenses that remain relatively constant regardless of how much revenue you're generating or how many customers you're serving. Examples of fixed costs might include:

- Rent or mortgage payments for your office or workspace
- Salaries for full-time employees
- Equipment or software licenses
- Insurance premiums
- Utilities and other overhead expenses

While some fixed costs are unavoidable, there are often ways to minimize them or find more cost-effective alternatives. For example:

- Instead of renting a dedicated office space, consider working from home or using a coworking space on an as-needed basis.
- Instead of hiring full-time employees right away, consider using freelancers or contractors for specific projects or tasks.
- Instead of purchasing expensive equipment or software outright, consider leasing or using open-source alternatives.

By keeping your fixed costs low, you can give yourself more flexibility and adaptability as you grow and evolve your business. You'll be better able to weather fluctuations in revenue or customer demand, and you'll have more resources available to invest in growth and innovation.

Outsource non-core functions

Another way to operate lean is to outsource non-core functions that are not essential to your core value proposition or competitive advantage. By focusing on what you do best and outsourcing the rest, you can stay nimble and efficient while still delivering high-quality products or services to your customers.

Examples of non-core functions that you might consider outsourcing include:

- Bookkeeping and accounting
- Customer support and service
- Marketing and advertising
- IT and technical support
- Human resources and recruiting

- Shipping and fulfillment

When outsourcing non-core functions, it's important to choose partners who are reliable, experienced, and aligned with your values and goals. Look for providers who have a track record of success in your industry or niche, and who can offer flexible and scalable solutions that can grow with your business over time.

It's also important to have clear communication and expectations with your outsourcing partners. Make sure you have detailed contracts or service level agreements in place that outline the scope of work, deliverables, timelines, and pricing. Set up regular check-ins or status updates to ensure that everyone is on the same page and working towards the same goals.

By outsourcing non-core functions strategically, you can free up more of your time and resources to focus on what matters most – delivering value to your customers and growing your business.

Manage your cash flow carefully

Another critical aspect of operating lean is managing your cash flow carefully. Cash flow refers to the amount of money coming into and going out of your business at any given time. Positive cash flow means you have more money coming in than going out, while negative cash flow means the opposite.

As a bootstrapped founder, it's essential to have a clear understanding of your cash flow at all times. This means keeping accurate and up-to-date financial records, forecasting your revenue and expenses, and making data-driven decisions about how to allocate your resources.

Here are some key strategies for managing your cash flow effectively:

- **Invoice promptly and follow up on late payments:** The faster you can get paid for your products or services, the better your cash flow will be. Make sure you have clear payment terms and policies in place, and don't be afraid to follow up with customers who are behind on payments.

- **Negotiate favorable payment terms with vendors and suppliers**: Look for opportunities to extend payment terms or get discounts for early payment. This can help you conserve cash and improve your overall cash flow.
- **Keep a close eye on your expenses:** Track your spending carefully and look for ways to cut costs or find more cost-effective alternatives. Avoid unnecessary expenses and be strategic about how you invest in growth and expansion.
- **Use a cash flow forecast to plan ahead:** A cash flow forecast is a tool that helps you project your future cash inflows and outflows based on historical data and assumptions about future revenue and expenses. By creating a cash flow forecast, you can identify potential cash shortages or surpluses in advance and make proactive decisions about how to manage your finances.
- **Consider using a line of credit or other financing options:** While taking on debt should always be done cautiously, having a line

of credit or other financing options available can help you smooth out cash flow fluctuations and invest in growth opportunities when needed.

By managing your cash flow carefully and making data-driven decisions about how to allocate your resources, you can ensure that your business has the financial stability and flexibility it needs to thrive over the long term.

Leverage automation and technology

Another way to operate lean and maximize your resources is to leverage automation and technology wherever possible. By using tools and platforms that streamline your processes and reduce manual labor, you can save time and money while still delivering high-quality products or services to your customers.

Examples of areas where you might consider leveraging automation and technology include:

Marketing and lead generation.

Use tools like email marketing platforms, social media schedulers, and chatbots to automate your outreach and engagement with potential customers.

Sales and customer relationship management

Use a CRM platform to track and manage your interactions with customers and prospects, and automate follow-up tasks and reminders.

Project management and collaboration

Use tools like Trello, Asana, or Basecamp to organize and track your projects, assign tasks, and collaborate with your team members.

Accounting and financial management

Use accounting software like QuickBooks or Xero to automate your bookkeeping and financial reporting, and connect your bank accounts and credit cards for real-time transaction tracking.

Customer support and service

Use a helpdesk platform like Zendesk or Freshdesk to manage customer inquiries and support tickets, and provide self-service resources like knowledge bases and FAQs.

When leveraging automation and technology, it's important to choose tools that are well-suited to your specific needs and workflow. Look for solutions that integrate seamlessly with your existing systems and processes, and that offer robust features and customization options.

It's also important to keep in mind that automation and technology are not a substitute for human interaction and expertise. While these tools can help you streamline and scale your operations, they should always be used in service of your larger goals and values as a business.

Foster a culture of frugality and resourcefulness

Finally, to truly operate lean and maximize your resources as a bootstrapped founder, it's important to foster a culture of frugality and resourcefulness throughout your organization. This means instilling a mindset of creativity, adaptability, and efficiency in yourself and your team members.

Here are some key ways to foster a culture of frugality and resourcefulness:

Lead by example

As the founder and leader of your business, it's important to model the behaviors and values you want to see in your team members. Be transparent about your financial goals and decisions, and show a willingness to make tough choices in the name of operating lean.

Celebrate creativity and innovation

Encourage your team members to think outside the box and come up with novel solutions to problems or challenges. Celebrate and reward ideas that help your business save money or operate more efficiently.

Emphasize the importance of ROI

When making decisions about investments or expenses, always consider the potential return on investment. Encourage your team members to think critically about how each decision will impact your bottom line and overall goals.

Foster a sense of ownership and accountability

Give your team members the autonomy and responsibility to make decisions and take ownership of their work. Hold everyone accountable for their contributions and impact on the business.

Embrace a growth mindset

Encourage your team members to continuously learn and improve their skills and knowledge. Provide opportunities for professional development and career growth, and celebrate progress and achievements along the way.

By fostering a culture of frugality and resourcefulness, you can create a team that is motivated, engaged, and committed to the success of your bootstrapped business. You'll be better able to weather challenges and setbacks, and you'll have the resilience and adaptability you need to thrive over the long term.

Final Thought

Operating lean is essential for bootstrapped founders who want to maximize their resources and minimize their risk as they scale their businesses over time. By keeping fixed costs low, outsourcing non-core functions, managing cash flow carefully, leveraging automation and technology, and fostering a culture of frugality and resourcefulness, you can create a business that is nimble, efficient, and well-positioned for long-term success.

Remember, operating lean is not about cutting corners or sacrificing quality — it's about being strategic and intentional about how you allocate your limited resources. By staying focused on your core value proposition and making data-driven decisions about how to grow and evolve your business, you can build a sustainable and profitable venture that can weather the ups and downs of the entrepreneurial journey.

In the next chapter, we'll explore some strategies for building and managing a small but mighty team as you scale your bootstrapped business. From hiring and onboarding to creating a strong culture and fostering employee engagement, we'll discuss how to build a team that is aligned with your values and goals and committed to your long-term success.

Chapter 9: Building a Small but Mighty Team and Creating a Strong Culture

As a bootstrapped founder, one of your most important tasks is to build and manage a team that can help you achieve your goals and grow your business over time. But with limited resources and a lean operating model, it can be challenging to know how to build a team that is both effective and efficient.

In this chapter, we'll explore some strategies for building a small but mighty team and creating a strong culture that can support your long-term success as a bootstrapped business. From hiring and onboarding to fostering employee engagement and development, we'll discuss how to create a team that is aligned with your values and goals and committed to your vision for the future.

Hire for fit and potential

When building a team as a bootstrapped founder, it's important to be strategic and selective about who you bring on board. With limited resources and a lean operating model, you can't afford to make hiring mistakes or bring on team members who are not a good fit for your culture and values.

One key strategy for building a strong team is to hire for fit and potential, rather than just skills and experience. While it's important to have team members with the necessary expertise and knowledge to do their jobs well, it's equally important to have team members who are aligned with your values and mission, and who have the potential to grow and evolve with your business over time.

When hiring for fit and potential, look for candidates who:

- **Share your values and vision for the business.** They should be excited about your mission and purpose, and committed to helping you achieve your goals.
- **Have a growth mindset and a willingness to learn.** They should be open to feedback and

eager to develop their skills and knowledge over time.

- **Are adaptable and resilient.** They should be able to handle change and uncertainty, and be willing to pivot or adjust their approach as needed.
- **Are proactive and self-motivated.** They should be able to take initiative and ownership of their work, and be willing to go above and beyond to deliver results.
- **Have strong communication and collaboration skills.** They should be able to work well with others, give and receive feedback, and contribute to a positive team dynamic.

By hiring for fit and potential, you can build a team that is not only skilled and experienced, but also aligned with your values and culture. This can help you create a more cohesive and effective team that is better able to weather challenges and setbacks, and deliver results for your business over time.

Onboard and train effectively

Once you've hired the right team members, it's important to onboard and train them effectively to set them up for success in their roles. Effective onboarding and training can help new team members feel welcome and supported, and give them the tools and knowledge they need to hit the ground running and contribute to your business right away.

Here are some key strategies for onboarding and training your team effectively:

- **Create a clear and comprehensive onboarding plan:** This should include an overview of your business, your values and culture, and the specific role and responsibilities of each new team member.
- **Provide hands-on training and support:** Give new team members the opportunity to shadow more experienced team members, attend training sessions or workshops, and receive ongoing coaching and feedback.

- **Set clear expectations and goals:** Make sure each team member understands what is expected of them in their role, and how their work contributes to the overall success of the business.
- **Foster a culture of continuous learning and development:** Encourage team members to seek out new skills and knowledge, and provide opportunities for ongoing training and professional development.
- **Celebrate milestones and achievements:** Recognize and reward team members for their hard work and contributions, and celebrate major milestones and successes along the way.

By investing in effective onboarding and training, you can help your team members feel valued and supported, and give them the tools and knowledge they need to succeed in their roles. This can lead to higher employee engagement, retention, and productivity over time.

Foster a culture of transparency and communication

Another key to building a strong and effective team is to foster a culture of transparency and communication. When team members feel informed and included in the decision-making process, they are more likely to be engaged and motivated to contribute to the success of the business.

Here are some strategies for fostering a culture of transparency and communication:

- **Share information openly and regularly:** Keep team members informed about the state of the business, including financial performance, major initiatives, and changes or challenges.
- **Encourage open and honest feedback:** Create a safe and supportive environment where team members feel comfortable sharing their thoughts, ideas, and concerns.
- **Hold regular team meetings and check-ins:** Use these opportunities to share updates,

celebrate successes, and discuss challenges or roadblocks.
- **Use collaboration tools and platforms:** Leverage tools like Slack, Google Docs, or Asana to facilitate communication and collaboration among team members.
- **Lead by example:** As the founder and leader of your business, it's important to model transparency and communication in your own interactions with team members.

By fostering a culture of transparency and communication, you can create a more engaged and motivated team that is better able to work together towards common goals. This can lead to better decision-making, problem-solving, and overall performance for your business.

Empower and trust your team

As a bootstrapped founder, it can be tempting to try to control every aspect of your business and micromanage your team members. But this approach can ultimately be counterproductive, leading to burnout, disengagement, and turnover among your team.

Instead, it's important to empower and trust your team members to take ownership of their work and make decisions that are in the best interest of the business. When team members feel trusted and valued, they are more likely to be motivated, engaged, and committed to their roles and the success of the business.

Here are some strategies for empowering and trusting your team:

- **Give team members autonomy and decision-making power.** Allow them to take ownership of their work and make decisions within their areas of expertise.
- **Provide clear expectations and guidelines.** Make sure team members understand the parameters within which they can operate, and the outcomes they are responsible for achieving.

- **Offer support and resources.** Give team members the tools, training, and support they need to succeed in their roles, and be available to provide guidance and feedback as needed.
- **Encourage experimentation and risk-taking.** Create a safe space for team members to try new things, make mistakes, and learn from their experiences.
- **Celebrate successes and learn from failures.** Recognize and reward team members for their achievements, and use failures as opportunities for learning and growth.

By empowering and trusting your team members, you can create a more engaged and motivated workforce that is better able to innovate, problem-solve, and deliver results for your business. This can lead to higher productivity, better decision-making, and a stronger overall culture of ownership and accountability.

Invest in employee development and growth

Finally, to build a truly strong and effective team, it's important to invest in employee development and growth over time. When team members feel supported and encouraged to grow and develop their skills and knowledge, they are more likely to be engaged, motivated, and committed to their roles and the success of the business.

Here are some strategies for investing in employee development and growth:

- **Provide ongoing training and development opportunities.** Offer workshops, seminars, or online courses that help team members develop new skills and knowledge relevant to their roles.
- **Encourage cross-functional collaboration and learning.** Create opportunities for team members to work with and learn from colleagues in other departments or areas of expertise.
- **Offer mentorship and coaching.** Pair more experienced team members with newer or less

experienced colleagues to provide guidance, support, and feedback.
- **Create career growth and advancement opportunities.** Provide clear paths for team members to advance within the organization, and offer opportunities for increased responsibility and leadership.
- **Recognize and reward growth and development.** Celebrate team members who take initiative to develop their skills and knowledge, and reward them with increased opportunities and compensation.

By investing in employee development and growth, you can create a team that is not only skilled and experienced, but also engaged, motivated, and committed to the long-term success of your business. This can lead to higher retention, better performance, and a stronger overall culture of learning and growth.

Final Thought

Building a small but mighty team is essential for bootstrapped founders who want to scale their businesses over time. By hiring for fit and potential, onboarding and training effectively, fostering a culture of transparency and communication, empowering and trusting your team, and investing in employee development and growth, you can create a team that is aligned with your values and goals, and committed to your long-term success.

Remember, building a strong team is not a one-time event – it's an ongoing process that requires continuous investment and attention. By staying focused on your team and their needs, and making intentional decisions about how to support and develop them over time, you can create a culture that attracts and retains top talent, and drives your business forward.

In the next chapter, we'll explore some strategies for overcoming challenges and staying resilient as a bootstrapped founder. From dealing with setbacks and failures to staying motivated and avoiding burnout, we'll discuss how to navigate the ups and downs of the entrepreneurial journey and build a business that can stand the test of time.

Chapter 10: Dealing with Setbacks and Pivoting When Necessary

As a bootstrapped founder, you will inevitably face setbacks and challenges along the way. Whether it's a product launch that falls flat, a key employee who leaves unexpectedly, or a market shift that disrupts your business model, there will be times when things don't go according to plan.

The key to overcoming these setbacks is to stay resilient, adaptable, and open to change. In this chapter, we'll explore some strategies for dealing with setbacks and pivoting when necessary to keep your business moving forward.

Embrace a growth mindset

One of the most important things you can do as a bootstrapped founder is to embrace a growth mindset. This means viewing setbacks and challenges not as failures, but as opportunities for learning and growth.

When you have a growth mindset, you see your abilities and intelligence as malleable and capable of improvement over time. You view effort and persistence as the keys to success, rather than innate talent or luck. And you approach challenges with a sense of curiosity and determination, rather than fear or avoidance.

Embracing a growth mindset can be especially important when dealing with setbacks and failures. Instead of getting discouraged or giving up, you can use these experiences as opportunities to learn, adapt, and improve. You can ask yourself questions like:

- What can I learn from this experience?
- How can I use this feedback to improve my product, my team, or my strategy?
- What new opportunities or insights have emerged as a result of this setback?

By reframing setbacks as opportunities for growth and learning, you can stay resilient and motivated even in the face of challenges. You can also model a growth mindset for your team, encouraging them to embrace challenges and learn from their mistakes as well.

Conduct a post-mortem analysis

When a setback or failure occurs, it's important to take the time to conduct a thorough post-mortem analysis. This means examining what went wrong, why it happened, and what you can learn from the experience to prevent similar issues in the future.

Here are some key steps to conducting a post-mortem analysis:

- **Gather data and feedback:** Collect as much information as possible about what happened, including data on key metrics, customer feedback, and team insights.
- **Identify the root causes:** Look beyond the surface-level symptoms to identify the underlying factors that contributed to the setback or failure. This could include issues

with product design, marketing strategy, team dynamics, or external market factors.

- **Brainstorm solutions:** Once you've identified the root causes, work with your team to brainstorm potential solutions or improvements. Be open to new ideas and approaches, and prioritize solutions that address the underlying issues rather than just the symptoms.
- **Create an action plan:** Turn your brainstormed solutions into a concrete action plan, with clear owners, timelines, and metrics for success. Make sure everyone on the team understands their role and responsibilities in implementing the plan.
- **Communicate and document:** Share the results of your post-mortem analysis with your team and stakeholders, and document the lessons learned for future reference. Use this as an opportunity to build transparency, accountability, and continuous improvement into your company culture.

By conducting a thorough post-mortem analysis after a setback or failure, you can turn a negative experience into a valuable learning opportunity. You can identify blind spots or weaknesses in your business, and take proactive steps to address them moving forward.

Be willing to pivot when necessary

Sometimes, despite your best efforts, a setback or failure may require a more significant change in direction. This is where the concept of pivoting comes in.

Pivoting means making a fundamental change to your business model, product, or target market in response to new information or changing circumstances. It's a way of adapting and evolving your business to better meet the needs of your customers and the realities of the market.

Some common reasons for pivoting include:

- **Lack of product-market fit.** If you're not seeing the traction or adoption you expected from your target customers, it may be time to rethink your product or market focus.

- **Changing customer needs or preferences.** If your customers' needs or behaviors have shifted, you may need to adjust your product or marketing strategy to stay relevant and competitive.
- **New market opportunities.** If you identify a new market or customer segment that represents a better fit for your business, pivoting to pursue that opportunity can be a smart move.
- **Unsustainable unit economics.** If your current business model is not generating enough revenue or profit to sustain growth, pivoting to a new pricing or cost structure may be necessary.

Pivoting can be a scary and uncertain process, but it can also be a powerful way to unlock new growth and opportunities for your business. The key is to approach pivoting with a clear strategy and a willingness to experiment and learn.

Here are some tips for successful pivoting:

- Start with customer feedback. Use data and insights from your customers to inform your pivoting decisions. Look for patterns or trends in their behavior or feedback that suggest a need for change.
- Test and validate. Before committing to a full pivot, test and validate your new approach with a small group of customers or users. Use their feedback to refine and improve your strategy before scaling up.
- Communicate clearly. Be transparent with your team, investors, and customers about the reasons for pivoting and the expected outcomes. Make sure everyone understands the new direction and their role in making it successful.
- Stay focused on your core strengths. While pivoting can involve significant changes, it's important to stay focused on your core strengths and values as a business. Look for ways to leverage your existing assets, expertise, and customer relationships in new and creative ways.
- Celebrate small wins. Pivoting can be a long and challenging process, so it's important to

celebrate small wins and milestones along the way. Recognize and reward your team for their hard work and adaptability, and use these moments to build momentum and motivation.

By being willing to pivot when necessary, you can stay agile and responsive in the face of changing market conditions and customer needs. You can also unlock new opportunities for growth and innovation that may not have been apparent before.

Build resilience through adversity

Ultimately, dealing with setbacks and pivoting when necessary is about building resilience as a bootstrapped founder and as a business. Resilience is the ability to bounce back from challenges and setbacks, and to adapt and thrive in the face of adversity.

Building resilience takes time and practice, but there are some key strategies you can use to cultivate this important quality:

- **Focus on your purpose and values.** When faced with setbacks or challenges, stay grounded in your core purpose and values as a business. Remember why you started your company in the first place, and let that sense of mission and impact guide your decisions and actions.
- **Cultivate a support network.** Surround yourself with mentors, advisors, and peers who can offer guidance, perspective, and emotional support during tough times. Don't be afraid to ask for help or advice when you need it.
-
- **Practice self-care.** As a founder, it's easy to get caught up in the day-to-day demands of running a business and neglect your own well-being. Make sure to prioritize self-care activities like exercise, meditation, and time with loved ones to maintain your physical and mental health.
- **Reframe challenges as opportunities.** Instead of viewing setbacks as failures or obstacles, try to reframe them as opportunities for learning, growth, and innovation. Look for

the silver lining in every challenge, and use it to fuel your motivation and creativity.
- **Celebrate successes and milestones.** Make sure to take time to celebrate your successes and milestones along the way, no matter how small they may seem. Recognizing and rewarding progress can help build momentum and motivation, and remind you of how far you've come.

By building resilience through adversity, you can develop the mental toughness and adaptability needed to navigate the ups and downs of bootstrapping a business. You can also inspire resilience in your team and stakeholders, creating a culture of perseverance and growth that can sustain your business over the long term.

Final Thought

Dealing with setbacks and pivoting when necessary is an essential skill for any bootstrapped founder. By embracing a growth mindset, conducting post-mortem analyses, being willing to pivot when needed, and building resilience through adversity, you can turn challenges into opportunities and keep your business moving forward.

Remember, setbacks and failures are not a reflection of your worth or abilities as a founder. They are simply part of the learning and growth process that comes with building a successful business. By staying focused on your purpose, surrounding yourself with support, and cultivating a resilient mindset, you can overcome any obstacle and achieve your entrepreneurial dreams.

Chapter 11: Competing with VC-Backed Companies by Focusing on Customer Loyalty and Sustainable Growth

As a bootstrapped founder, you may often find yourself competing with well-funded, VC-backed companies in your market. These companies may have more resources, larger teams, and bigger marketing budgets, which can make it feel like an uphill battle to win customers and grow your business.

However, there are some key advantages that bootstrapped companies have over their VC-backed counterparts. By focusing on customer loyalty, sustainable growth, and long-term value creation, you can differentiate yourself in the market and build a business that can thrive without relying on external funding.

In this chapter, we'll explore some strategies for competing with VC-backed companies by leveraging your unique strengths as a bootstrapped founder.

Focus on customer loyalty and retention

One of the biggest advantages that bootstrapped companies have over VC-backed companies is the ability to focus on customer loyalty and retention. When you're not beholden to external investors or growth targets, you can prioritize building deep, long-term relationships with your customers and delivering exceptional value over time.

Here are some strategies for building customer loyalty and retention as a bootstrapped founder:

- **Prioritize customer service and support.** Make sure to invest in high-quality customer service and support, and go above and beyond to solve customer problems and address their needs. Respond quickly to inquiries and complaints, and proactively reach out to customers to gather feedback and insights.
- **Personalize the customer experience.** Use data and insights to personalize the customer experience and make each interaction feel tailored to their individual needs and preferences. This could include personalized

product recommendations, customized onboarding flows, or targeted marketing messages.

- **Build a community around your brand.** Encourage customers to connect with each other and with your brand through online forums, social media groups, or in-person events. Foster a sense of belonging and shared purpose among your customer base, and make them feel like valued members of your community.

- **Offer loyalty programs and rewards.** Implement loyalty programs or rewards systems that incentivize customers to continue doing business with you over time. This could include discounts, exclusive perks, or other benefits that recognize and reward their loyalty and engagement.

- **Continuously improve the product and user experience.** Keep investing in product development and user experience improvements based on customer feedback and changing needs. Show customers that you're committed to delivering the best possible experience and value over time, and that their input and feedback matter.

By focusing on customer loyalty and retention, you can build a stable and sustainable customer base that can help you weather market fluctuations and competitive pressures. You can also create a virtuous cycle of positive word-of-mouth and referrals that can help you acquire new customers organically over time.

Emphasize sustainable growth and profitability

Another key advantage of bootstrapping is the ability to prioritize sustainable growth and profitability over rapid scaling and market share gains. While VC-backed companies may be under pressure to grow at all costs and achieve a quick exit, bootstrapped founders have the flexibility to take a more measured and strategic approach to growth.

Here are some strategies for emphasizing sustainable growth and profitability as a bootstrapped founder:

- **Focus on unit economics and margins.** Make sure to have a clear understanding of your unit economics and profit margins, and prioritize initiatives that can improve these metrics over time. Look for ways to optimize pricing, reduce costs, and increase efficiency across your business.
- **Reinvest profits into the business.** Instead of taking money off the table or pursuing an early exit, reinvest profits back into the business to fuel sustainable growth and innovation. Use these funds to hire key talent, develop new products or features, or expand into new markets.
- **Prioritize organic growth over paid acquisition.** While paid advertising can be an effective way to acquire customers quickly, it can also be expensive and unsustainable over the long term. Focus instead on organic growth strategies like content marketing, SEO, and referral programs that can help you attract customers naturally over time.
- **Build strategic partnerships and alliances.** Look for opportunities to partner with other companies or organizations that can help you

expand your reach, access new markets, or deliver complementary products or services. These partnerships can help you grow your business in a more sustainable and cost-effective way than going it alone.

- **Stay focused on your core strengths and values.** Don't get distracted by shiny objects or short-term opportunities that don't align with your long-term vision and values as a business. Stay focused on your core strengths and differentiators, and use these to guide your growth and innovation strategies over time.

By emphasizing sustainable growth and profitability, you can build a business that is resilient, adaptable, and built to last. You can also create a culture of financial discipline and strategic decision-making that can help you navigate the ups and downs of the market and emerge stronger over time.

Differentiate through unique value proposition and customer experience

In a crowded and competitive market, differentiation is key to standing out and winning customers. As a bootstrapped founder, you may not have the resources to compete head-to-head with larger, well-funded competitors on price or features alone. However, you can differentiate yourself through a unique value proposition and customer experience that sets you apart and resonates with your target audience.

Here are some strategies for differentiating through unique value proposition and customer experience:

- **Identify your unique selling proposition (USP).** Take the time to clearly articulate what makes your product, service, or brand unique and valuable to your target customers. This could be a specific feature, benefit, or approach that sets you apart from competitors and addresses a key pain point or need for your audience.
- **Develop a strong brand identity and messaging.** Use your USP as the foundation for a strong and consistent brand identity and messaging strategy. Develop a clear and compelling brand story, visual identity, and tone

of voice that communicates your unique value and resonates with your target audience.

- **Create a memorable and delightful customer experience.** Look for ways to create a customer experience that is not just functional, but memorable and delightful. This could include personalized touches, unexpected surprises, or exceptional service that goes above and beyond expectations.
- **Leverage customer feedback and insights.** Use customer feedback and insights to continuously improve and refine your value proposition and customer experience over time. Seek out opportunities to gather feedback through surveys, interviews, or user testing, and use this input to guide your product development and marketing strategies.
- **Emphasize your mission and values.** If your business is driven by a strong mission or set of values, use this as a differentiator and selling point with customers. Communicate your commitment to social responsibility, sustainability, or other causes that align with your brand and resonate with your target audience.

By differentiating through unique value proposition and customer experience, you can create a strong and compelling reason for customers to choose your business over competitors. You can also build a loyal and engaged customer base that is more likely to stick with you over the long term and advocate for your brand to others.

Leverage agility and adaptability

Finally, one of the key advantages of bootstrapping is the ability to be agile and adaptable in the face of changing market conditions and customer needs. Without the constraints of external investors or rigid growth targets, bootstrapped founders have the flexibility to pivot quickly, experiment with new ideas, and respond to new opportunities as they arise.

Here are some strategies for leveraging agility and adaptability as a bootstrapped founder:

- **Embrace a lean and iterative approach.** Use lean startup principles and agile methodologies to develop and test new products, features, and marketing strategies quickly and efficiently. Focus on rapid prototyping, user feedback, and data-driven decision making to guide your iterations and improvements over time.

- **Stay close to your customers and market.** Make sure to stay connected to your customers and market through regular feedback loops, user research, and competitive analysis. Use this input to stay ahead of changing needs and preferences, and adapt your strategies accordingly.
- **Foster a culture of experimentation and learning.** Encourage a culture of experimentation and continuous learning within your team. Empower employees to try new things, take calculated risks, and learn from both successes and failures. Use postmortems and retrospectives to capture lessons learned and apply them to future initiatives.
- **Be willing to pivot when necessary.** As we discussed in the previous chapter, be willing to pivot your business model, product, or target market when necessary based on new information or changing circumstances. Don't be afraid to make bold changes if they align

with your long-term vision and values as a business.

- **Leverage partnerships and collaborations.** Look for opportunities to partner with other startups, organizations, or thought leaders in your industry to expand your capabilities, reach new audiences, or tackle complex challenges together. These collaborations can help you stay agile and responsive to new opportunities without having to build everything yourself.

By leveraging agility and adaptability, you can stay ahead of the curve in a rapidly changing market and respond quickly to new opportunities and challenges as they arise. You can also foster a culture of innovation and continuous improvement that can help you outmaneuver larger, slower-moving competitors over time.

Final Thought

Competing with well-funded, VC-backed companies can be a daunting challenge for bootstrapped founders. However, by focusing on customer loyalty, sustainable growth, differentiation, and agility, you can level the playing field and build a business that can thrive without relying on external funding.

Remember, your biggest advantage as a bootstrapped founder is your ability to stay true to your vision, values, and customers over the long term. By prioritizing these key areas and staying focused on delivering exceptional value and experience to your target audience, you can build a loyal and engaged customer base that can help you weather any storm and emerge stronger over time.

Chapter 12: Avoiding Burnout and Maintaining Balance

As a bootstrapped founder, the pressure to succeed can be intense. Without the safety net of external funding or a large team to lean on, it can feel like the weight of the entire business is on your shoulders. This pressure, combined with the long hours and constant demands of running a startup, can lead to burnout and other mental health challenges if not managed properly.

In this chapter, we'll explore some strategies for avoiding burnout and maintaining balance as a bootstrapped founder. By prioritizing self-care, setting boundaries, and cultivating a supportive network, you can build a sustainable and fulfilling entrepreneurial journey that doesn't compromise your well-being or relationships.

Recognize the signs of burnout

The first step in avoiding burnout is recognizing the signs and symptoms before they become too severe.

Burnout is a state of chronic stress and exhaustion that can manifest in a variety of physical, emotional, and cognitive symptoms, such as:

Physical symptoms:

- - Fatigue and exhaustion
- - Headaches or muscle pain
- - Changes in appetite or sleep patterns
- - Weakened immune system and frequent illnesses

Emotional symptoms:

- - Feelings of cynicism, detachment, or apathy towards work
- - Irritability, frustration, or anger
- - Anxiety, depression, or mood swings
- - Loss of motivation or sense of accomplishment

Cognitive symptoms:

- - Difficulty concentrating or making decisions
- - Memory problems or forgetfulness
- - Negative or pessimistic thinking patterns
- - Lack of creativity or problem-solving skills

If you notice any of these symptoms in yourself or your team members, it's important to take action before they escalate into more serious health problems or impact your business performance.

Set realistic expectations and boundaries

One of the biggest contributors to burnout is the pressure to work long hours and be available 24/7. As a founder, it can be tempting to put in extra time and effort to get your business off the ground, but this is not sustainable over the long term.

To avoid burnout, it's important to set realistic expectations and boundaries around your work schedule and availability. This means:

- Establishing clear working hours and sticking to them as much as possible

- Taking regular breaks throughout the day to recharge and refocus
- Setting aside time for personal hobbies, interests, and relationships outside of work
- Communicating your availability and response times to team members and customers
- Delegating tasks and responsibilities to other team members when possible
- Learning to say no to non-essential requests or opportunities that don't align with your priorities

By setting clear boundaries and expectations, you can create a more sustainable and balanced work environment that allows you to show up as your best self both in and out of the office.

Prioritize self-care and stress management

In addition to setting boundaries, it's important to prioritize self-care and stress management as a bootstrapped founder. This means taking proactive steps to manage your physical, emotional, and mental well-being, even when you're busy or under pressure.

Some strategies for prioritizing self-care and stress management include:

- **Exercise and physical activity:** Regular exercise can help reduce stress, boost energy and mood, and improve overall health and well-being. Find an activity that you enjoy and make it a non-negotiable part of your routine, even if it's just a short walk or yoga session each day.
- **Healthy eating and sleep habits:** Fueling your body with nutritious foods and getting enough quality sleep can help you stay focused, energized, and resilient in the face of stress. Make sure to prioritize healthy meals and snacks, limit caffeine and alcohol intake, and aim for 7-9 hours of sleep each night.
- **Mindfulness and relaxation techniques:** Incorporating mindfulness practices like meditation, deep breathing, or journaling can help you stay grounded and manage stress in the moment. Take short breaks throughout the day to practice these techniques and give your mind a chance to reset and recharge.

- **Hobbies and creative outlets:** Engaging in hobbies or creative pursuits outside of work can help you maintain a sense of joy and fulfillment, even when work is stressful. Make time for activities that you enjoy and that allow you to express yourself in different ways, whether it's painting, playing music, or gardening.
- **Social support and connection:** Building a strong network of supportive friends, family members, and colleagues can help you feel less isolated and overwhelmed as a founder. Make time for regular social connections and don't be afraid to reach out for help or advice when you need it.

By prioritizing self-care and stress management, you can build resilience and maintain a sense of balance and well-being even in the face of entrepreneurial challenges.

Cultivate a supportive network and seek help when needed

Another key strategy for avoiding burnout and maintaining balance is to cultivate a supportive network of mentors, advisors, and peers who can offer guidance, perspective, and encouragement along the way.

As a bootstrapped founder, it can be easy to feel like you're in it alone, but the reality is that there are many people who have been in your shoes and who are willing to help. Here are some ways to build and leverage a supportive network:

- **Join a startup community or accelerator program:** Participating in a startup community or accelerator can help you connect with other founders, mentors, and investors who can offer advice, feedback, and resources. Look for programs that align with your industry or stage of growth and take advantage of networking and educational opportunities.
- **Seek out mentors and advisors:** Identify experienced entrepreneurs or experts in your industry who can serve as mentors or advisors to your business. Reach out to them for guidance on specific challenges or decisions, and be open to their feedback and perspective.

- **Build relationships with other founders Build relationships with other founders:** Connecting with other founders who are at a similar stage or facing similar challenges can be a valuable source of support and camaraderie. Attend industry events, join online forums or social media groups, and look for opportunities to collaborate or share resources with other founders in your network.
- **Hire coaches or consultants:** If you're struggling with a particular area of your business or personal development, consider hiring a coach or consultant who can provide targeted guidance and support. This could be a business coach, a leadership coach, or a mental health professional who specializes in working with entrepreneurs.
- **Ask for help when you need it:** Finally, don't be afraid to ask for help when you need it, whether it's from your team members, advisors, or personal support network. Admitting that you need support is not a sign of weakness, but rather a sign of self-awareness and proactive problem-solving.

By cultivating a supportive network and seeking help when needed, you can access valuable resources, perspective, and encouragement to help you navigate the ups and downs of bootstrapping.

Celebrate successes and milestones along the way

Finally, one of the most important strategies for avoiding burnout and maintaining balance is to celebrate your successes and milestones along the way. As a bootstrapped founder, it can be easy to get caught up in the day-to-day challenges and forget to acknowledge the progress and achievements you've made.

Taking time to celebrate your wins, no matter how small, can help you maintain a sense of momentum, motivation, and purpose in your work. Here are some ways to celebrate successes and milestones:

- **Set specific, measurable goals and track your progress:** Break down your larger vision into specific, measurable goals and track your progress towards them over time. Celebrate when you hit key milestones or achieve important objectives, and use these moments to reflect on how far you've come.

- **Share your wins with your team and supporters:** Don't keep your successes to yourself - share them with your team members, advisors, and supporters who have helped you along the way. Acknowledge their contributions and celebrate together as a group.
- **Take time for reflection and gratitude:** Set aside regular time for reflection and gratitude, whether it's through journaling, meditation, or simply taking a few moments each day to appreciate the good things in your life and work. This can help you maintain a positive outlook and avoid getting bogged down in stress and negativity.
- **Reward yourself and your team for hard work:** When you or your team members go above and beyond or achieve something significant, take time to reward and recognize that effort. This could be through bonuses, extra time off, or simply a heartfelt thank-you and acknowledgement of their hard work.

- **Celebrate the journey, not just the destination:** Finally, remember to celebrate the journey itself, not just the end goal. Building a successful bootstrapped business is a long and challenging process, and every step along the way is an accomplishment worth recognizing and appreciating.

By celebrating your successes and milestones along the way, you can maintain a sense of progress, purpose, and motivation in your work, even when things get tough.

Final Thought

Avoiding burnout and maintaining balance is essential for bootstrapped founders who want to build sustainable and fulfilling businesses over the long term. By recognizing the signs of burnout, setting realistic expectations and boundaries, prioritizing self-care and stress management, cultivating a supportive network, and celebrating successes along the way, you can create a more balanced and resilient approach to entrepreneurship.

Remember, building a successful bootstrapped business is not a sprint, but a marathon. It requires patience, perseverance, and a willingness to adapt and grow over time. By taking care of yourself and your team, staying focused on your vision and values, and celebrating your progress along the way, you can create a business and a life that you love, without sacrificing your health or well-being in the process.

Chapter 13: Growing Sustainably by Reinvesting Profits and Scaling Responsibly

As a bootstrapped founder, one of the most important decisions you'll face as your business grows is how to reinvest your profits and scale your operations in a sustainable way. Without the pressure of external investors or the temptation of quick exits, you have the opportunity to build a business that can thrive over the long term, creating value for your customers, your team, and yourself.

In this chapter, we'll explore some strategies for growing sustainably by reinvesting profits and scaling responsibly. By taking a disciplined and strategic approach to growth, you can build a business that is resilient, adaptable, and built to last.

Reinvest profits into the business

One of the key advantages of bootstrapping is that you have complete control over how you allocate your profits. Instead of being beholden to the demands of external investors or the pressure to deliver short-term returns, you can reinvest your profits back into the business to fuel long-term growth and sustainability.

Here are some ways to reinvest profits into your business:

- **Invest in research and development:** Use your profits to fund research and development initiatives that can help you improve your products, services, or processes. This could include investing in new technologies, conducting market research, or hiring specialized talent to drive innovation.
- **Expand your team and capabilities:** As your business grows, you may need to expand your team and capabilities to keep up with demand and take on new opportunities. Use your profits to hire key roles, such as salespeople, marketers, or developers, and invest in training and development programs to help your team grow and succeed.
- **Improve your infrastructure and systems:** Reinvesting profits into your infrastructure and systems can help you scale more efficiently and

effectively. This could include upgrading your software and hardware, automating processes, or investing in customer support and service tools.

- **Acquire complementary businesses or assets:** If you identify an opportunity to acquire a complementary business or asset that can help you expand your market share, enter new markets, or improve your offerings, consider using your profits to fund the acquisition. Be sure to conduct thorough due diligence and have a clear integration plan in place.
- **Invest in marketing and customer acquisition:** While organic growth is ideal, there may be times when investing in paid marketing and customer acquisition can help you reach new audiences and drive growth. Use your profits to test and scale marketing campaigns that deliver a positive return on investment and align with your overall growth strategy.

By reinvesting your profits back into the business, you can create a virtuous cycle of growth and sustainability. As your business becomes more profitable and efficient, you'll have more resources to invest in innovation, expansion, and improvement, which in turn can drive even greater profitability and growth over time.

Scale responsibly and strategically

While reinvesting profits is important, it's equally important to scale your business responsibly and strategically. Scaling too quickly or haphazardly can lead to quality issues, customer churn, and financial instability, while scaling too slowly can cause you to miss out on important opportunities and fall behind competitors.

Here are some strategies for scaling responsibly and strategically:

- **Define your growth objectives and metrics:** Before you start scaling, define clear growth objectives and metrics that align with your overall business strategy. This could include revenue targets, customer acquisition goals, or

product development milestones. Use these objectives to guide your scaling efforts and track your progress over time.
- **Prioritize scalable processes and systems:** As you scale, it's important to have processes and systems in place that can handle increased volume and complexity. Prioritize developing scalable processes for key functions such as sales, marketing, customer service, and operations, and invest in tools and technologies that can help you automate and streamline these processes.
- **Focus on your core strengths and differentiators:** As you scale, it can be tempting to try to be everything to everyone. However, this can lead to a lack of focus and dilution of your brand and value proposition. Instead, focus on your core strengths and differentiators - the things that make your business unique and valuable to your target customers. Double down on these areas and use them to guide your scaling efforts.
- **Build a strong and adaptable team:** Scaling successfully requires a strong and adaptable team that can handle the challenges and

opportunities of growth. Invest in hiring, training, and retaining top talent, and foster a culture of collaboration, innovation, and continuous learning. Empower your team members to take ownership of their roles and contribute to the company's growth and success.

- **Test and iterate as you grow:** Scaling is not a one-time event, but an ongoing process of testing, learning, and iterating. As you implement new processes, systems, or strategies, be sure to track your results and gather feedback from your team and customers. Use this data to make informed decisions about what's working and what needs to be improved, and be willing to pivot or adjust your approach as needed.

By scaling responsibly and strategically, you can build a business that is efficient, effective, and positioned for long-term success. You'll be able to capitalize on new opportunities and navigate challenges with confidence, while staying true to your core values and delivering value to your customers.

Balance growth with profitability

One of the biggest challenges of scaling a bootstrapped business is balancing growth with profitability. While it's important to invest in growth initiatives that can help you expand your market share and revenue, it's equally important to ensure that your business remains profitable and financially stable along the way.

Here are some strategies for balancing growth with profitability:

- **Monitor your key financial metrics:** Keep a close eye on your key financial metrics, such as revenue, expenses, cash flow, and profit margins. Use this data to make informed decisions about where to invest your resources and where to cut costs or optimize efficiency. Set financial targets and benchmarks, and track your progress towards them over time.
- **Prioritize high-margin offerings:** As you scale, focus on developing and promoting offerings that have high profit margins and strong customer demand. This could include

premium products or services, add-on features,
or recurring revenue streams. By prioritizing
high-margin offerings, you can increase your
overall profitability and generate more cash
flow to reinvest into the business.

- **Optimize your pricing and cost structure:**
Regularly review and optimize your pricing and
cost structure to ensure that you're maximizing
profitability while remaining competitive in the
market. Look for opportunities to reduce costs
through automation, outsourcing, or
negotiating better terms with suppliers, and
adjust your pricing based on market demand
and customer value.

- **Focus on customer retention and loyalty:**
Acquiring new customers can be expensive, so
it's important to focus on retaining and
delighting your existing customers as you scale.
Invest in customer success and support
initiatives, develop loyalty programs and referral
incentives, and continuously gather feedback
and insights to improve the customer
experience. By building a loyal and engaged
customer base, you can increase your lifetime
value per customer and reduce your overall
acquisition costs.

Be willing to say no to unprofitable opportunities: As you scale, you may be presented with a variety of opportunities and partnerships that seem exciting but may not be profitable or aligned with your overall strategy. Be willing to say no to these opportunities, even if they seem like quick wins in the short term. Stay focused on your core business and your long-term goals, and only pursue opportunities that have a clear path to profitability and strategic value.

By balancing growth with profitability, you can build a business that is both financially sustainable and positioned for long-term success. You'll be able to invest in the right initiatives at the right time, while maintaining a healthy cash flow and bottom line.

Plan for the long term

Finally, as a bootstrapped founder, it's important to plan for the long term and build a business that can stand the test of time. While the allure of quick exits or overnight successes may be tempting, the reality is that building a sustainable and impactful business takes time, perseverance, and a long-term perspective.

Here are some strategies for planning for the long term:

- **Define your mission and values:** Start by defining your company's mission and values - the guiding principles that will shape your decisions and actions over the long term. Your mission should articulate the impact you want to have on the world and the value you want to create for your customers and stakeholders. Your values should reflect the behaviors and attitudes that you want to cultivate within your team and your business.
- **Create a long-term vision and roadmap:** Based on your mission and values, create a long-term vision for your business - a compelling picture of what your business could look like in 5, 10, or even 20 years. Use this vision to create a strategic roadmap that outlines the key milestones and initiatives you'll need to pursue over time to achieve your goals. Break this roadmap down into shorter-term objectives and tactics, and use it to guide your decision-making and resource allocation.

- **Build a strong and sustainable company culture:** As you grow and scale your business, it's important to build a strong and sustainable company culture that reflects your values and attracts top talent. Invest in developing your leadership skills and creating a positive and inclusive work environment that empowers your team members to do their best work. Foster open communication, transparency, and accountability, and create opportunities for growth and development within the company.
- **Plan for succession and continuity:** As a founder, it's important to plan for your own succession and the continuity of your business over the long term. This could include developing a strong leadership team that can take over key responsibilities, creating a clear ownership and governance structure, and putting in place legal and financial protections to ensure the business can continue to thrive even if you're no longer involved.
- **Continuously learn and adapt:** Finally, remember that building a successful business is a continuous process of learning and adaptation. As the market, your customers, and

your own needs and goals evolve over time, be willing to reassess your strategies and approaches and make changes as needed. Stay curious, stay open to new ideas and perspectives, and embrace the challenges and opportunities that come with long-term growth and success.

By planning for the long term and building a business that is mission-driven, values-aligned, and built to last, you can create a legacy that goes beyond just financial success. You can make a positive impact on the world, create meaningful jobs and opportunities for others, and build a business that you can be proud of for years to come.

Final Thought

Growing sustainably and scaling responsibly is one of the most important challenges facing bootstrapped founders as their businesses mature and evolve. By reinvesting profits strategically, scaling in a disciplined and focused way, balancing growth with profitability, and planning for the long term, you can build a business that is resilient, adaptable, and positioned for enduring success.

Remember, the path to sustainable growth is not always easy or straightforward. It requires hard work, perseverance, and a willingness to make tough decisions and trade-offs along the way. But by staying true to your values, focusing on your customers and your team, and maintaining a long-term perspective, you can navigate the challenges and opportunities of growth with confidence and purpose.

In the final chapter, we'll explore the importance of staying true to your vision and building a legacy business that can make a lasting impact on the world. We'll discuss strategies for maintaining your authenticity and purpose as you grow, and for creating a business that is not just successful, but truly meaningful and fulfilling.

Chapter 14: Staying True to Your Vision and Building a Legacy Business

As a bootstrapped founder, one of the most rewarding aspects of building a successful business is the opportunity to create something that is truly authentic to your vision and values. Unlike businesses that are beholden to external investors or the pressures of short-term returns, bootstrapped businesses have the freedom and flexibility to pursue a path that is guided by a deeper sense of purpose and meaning.

However, as businesses grow and scale, it can be easy to lose sight of this original vision and purpose. The demands of day-to-day operations, the pressure to hit growth targets, and the influence of outside stakeholders can all contribute to a sense of drift or misalignment over time.

In this final chapter, we'll explore some strategies for staying true to your vision and building a legacy business that can make a lasting impact on the world. We'll discuss how to maintain your authenticity and purpose as you grow, how to create a business that is truly meaningful and fulfilling, and how to build a legacy that goes beyond just financial success.

Define your purpose and values

The first step in staying true to your vision and building a legacy business is to clearly define your purpose and values. Your purpose is the reason why your business exists - the impact you want to have on the world and the value you want to create for your customers and stakeholders. Your values are the guiding principles that shape your decisions, actions, and behaviors as a business and as individuals within that business.

Here are some questions to consider when defining your purpose and values:

- What problem are you trying to solve or what need are you trying to meet?
- Who are you trying to serve and how do you want to make their lives better?

- What unique strengths, expertise, or perspective do you bring to the market?
- What do you stand for as a business and as individuals within that business?
- What kind of culture and work environment do you want to create?
- What impact do you want to have on your industry, your community, and the world?

By answering these questions and articulating your purpose and values clearly and concisely, you can create a north star that guides your business and keeps you aligned with your original vision over time.

Communicate and embed your purpose and values

Once you've defined your purpose and values, it's important to communicate them consistently and embed them deeply within your business. This means going beyond just putting them on a poster or a website, and actually living and breathing them in every aspect of your operations and culture.

Here are some ways to communicate and embed your purpose and values:

- **Incorporate them into your branding and messaging:** Use your purpose and values to shape your brand identity, messaging, and marketing efforts. Make sure that everything you communicate to the outside world is aligned with and reinforces your core purpose and values.
- **Make them a part of your hiring and onboarding process:** When hiring new team members, look for individuals who share your purpose and values and who are excited about contributing to your mission. During onboarding, make sure to clearly communicate your purpose and values and help new hires understand how their work contributes to the larger vision.
- **Reinforce them through your policies and practices:** Make sure that your company policies, procedures, and practices are aligned with and support your purpose and values Here are some additional ways to communicate and embed your purpose and values:

- **Celebrate and reward behaviors that align with your values:** When you see team members demonstrating behaviors or actions that align with your purpose and values, celebrate and reward them publicly. This could include shout-outs in team meetings, bonus programs, or other forms of recognition that reinforce the importance of living your values.
- **Make them a part of your decision-making process:** When facing difficult decisions or trade-offs, use your purpose and values as a lens through which to evaluate your options. Ask yourself which path is most aligned with your core purpose and values, and use that as a guide for making the right choice.
- **Continuously reinforce and evolve them over time:** As your business grows and evolves, make sure to continuously reinforce and evolve your purpose and values to keep them relevant and meaningful. Engage your team in regular discussions and reflections on how you're living your values, and be open to feedback and suggestions for improvement.

By communicating and embedding your purpose and values deeply within your business, you can create a culture and an organization that is truly authentic to your vision and that can withstand the challenges and pressures of growth and change over time.

Focus on creating value, not just wealth

Another key aspect of staying true to your vision and building a legacy business is to focus on creating value, not just wealth. While financial success is certainly important and necessary for the sustainability of your business, it should not be the sole or primary driver of your decision-making and actions.

Instead, focus on creating real, meaningful value for your customers, your team, your community, and the world at large. This could include:

- Developing products or services that solve real problems and meet genuine needs
- Creating jobs and opportunities that allow people to grow, learn, and thrive

- Contributing to the economic and social well-being of your local community
- Advancing important causes or movements that align with your purpose and values
- Pushing your industry forward through innovation, thought leadership, and positive change

By focusing on creating value in these ways, you can build a business that is not just financially successful, but also deeply meaningful and impactful. You can create a legacy that goes beyond just your own personal wealth and success, and that contributes to the greater good of society as a whole.

Build a strong and sustainable culture

Another critical component of building a legacy business is to create a strong and sustainable culture that can endure over time. Your culture is the set of shared values, beliefs, behaviors, and norms that define how your team works together and interacts with the outside world. It is the invisible glue that holds your organization together and shapes its character and identity.

To build a strong and sustainable culture, consider the following strategies:

- **Define and articulate your cultural values:** Just like your purpose and values, your cultural values should be clearly defined and articulated. These are the specific behaviors and attitudes that you want to cultivate within your team, such as transparency, collaboration, innovation, or customer-centricity.
- **Hire and develop people who align with your culture:** When hiring new team members, look for individuals who not only have the skills and experience you need, but also share your cultural values and fit well with your team. Invest in developing your existing team members and helping them grow and thrive within your culture.
- **Foster open communication and transparency:** Encourage open and honest communication within your team, and create channels and opportunities for people to share

their ideas, feedback, and concerns. Be transparent about your decision-making processes and the challenges and opportunities facing the business.

- **Celebrate and reinforce your culture regularly:** Look for ways to celebrate and reinforce your culture on a regular basis, whether through team-building activities, recognition programs, or other forms of engagement. Make sure that your cultural values are not just words on a wall, but are actively lived and practiced every day.
- **Evolve and adapt your culture over time:** As your business grows and changes, your culture will need to evolve and adapt as well. Be open to feedback and suggestions from your team, and be willing to make changes and improvements as needed to keep your culture strong and relevant.

By building a strong and sustainable culture, you can create an organization that is resilient, adaptable, and able to thrive over the long term. You can attract and retain top talent, foster innovation and creativity, and build deep and lasting relationships with your customers and stakeholders.

Plan for succession and continuity

Finally, to truly build a legacy business that can endure over time, it's important to plan for succession and continuity. This means thinking beyond your own personal involvement and ensuring that the business can continue to thrive and grow even when you're no longer at the helm.

Here are some strategies for planning for succession and continuity:

- **Develop a strong leadership team:** Invest in developing a strong and capable leadership team that can take on increasing levels of responsibility and decision-making over time. Look for individuals who share your vision and values, and who have the skills and experience needed to lead the business into the future.
- **Create a clear ownership and governance structure:** Make sure that you have a clear and

well-defined ownership and governance structure in place, with clear roles and responsibilities for key stakeholders such as founders, investors, and board members. Consider creating a succession plan that outlines how ownership and leadership will transition over time.

- **Document your processes and systems:** To ensure continuity and consistency over time, make sure to document your key processes, systems, and ways of working. Create standard operating procedures, knowledge bases, and other forms of documentation that can be used to onboard and train new team members and ensure that important information is not lost or forgotten.

- **Foster a culture of leadership and empowerment:** Encourage a culture of leadership and empowerment within your organization, where individuals at all levels are encouraged to take ownership and initiative. Create opportunities for people to develop their leadership skills and take on increasing levels of responsibility over time.

- **Consider your personal and financial planning:** As a founder, it's important to consider your own personal and financial planning as part of your succession and continuity strategy. This could include estate planning, wealth management, and other forms of long-term financial planning to ensure that you and your family are taken care of and that your business can continue to thrive.

By planning for succession and continuity, you can ensure that your business is built to last and that your legacy can endure long beyond your own personal involvement. You can create an organization that is resilient, adaptable, and able to continue creating value and making a positive impact on the world for generations to come.

Final Thought

Building a legacy business that stays true to your vision and values is one of the most rewarding and fulfilling aspects of being a bootstrapped founder. By defining your purpose and values, communicating and embedding them deeply within your organization, focusing on creating value, building a strong and sustainable culture, and planning for succession and continuity, you can create a business that is authentic, meaningful, and built to last.

Remember, building a legacy business is not just about financial success or personal achievement. It's about creating something that is larger than yourself and that can make a positive impact on the world. It's about leaving a lasting legacy that you can be proud of and that can continue to create value and meaning for generations to come.

As you continue on your journey as a bootstrapped founder, keep these principles and strategies in mind. Stay true to your vision and values, focus on creating real value for your customers and stakeholders, and build an organization that can endure and thrive over the long term. By doing so, you can create a business and a legacy that you can be truly proud of.

Conclusion

Congratulations! You've made it to the end of "Bootstrapping Your Way to Success: Building a Business Without VC". Throughout this book, we've explored the many challenges and opportunities that come with bootstrapping a business from the ground up, and we've provided a comprehensive roadmap for navigating this exciting and rewarding journey.

We started by laying the foundation for success, discussing the mindset and planning required to build a business without external funding. We emphasized the importance of choosing the right idea, one that aligns with your skills, passions, and the needs of the market. We also highlighted the value of creating a lean business plan and setting clear, measurable goals to guide your efforts.

Next, we dove into the tactical aspects of starting small and smart. We explored various funding options available to bootstrappers, from personal savings and credit cards to grants and customer funding. We discussed how to build a minimum viable product

(MVP) with limited resources, focusing on your core value proposition and testing your riskiest assumptions. We also provided strategies for marketing your business on a budget, leveraging grassroots tactics, social media, and networking to get the word out and attract your first customers.

As your business begins to gain traction, we shifted our focus to scaling up without breaking the bank. We emphasized the importance of generating revenue early and often, through tactics like pre-sales, subscriptions, and multiple revenue streams. We provided guidance on operating lean, keeping costs low, outsourcing strategically, and managing your cash flow carefully. We also discussed how to build a small but mighty team and create a strong company culture that can support your growth over time.

Of course, the path to bootstrapping success is rarely smooth or straightforward. We dedicated a section of the book to overcoming common challenges and staying resilient in the face of adversity. We discussed how to deal with setbacks and pivot your business when necessary, staying agile and adaptable to changing market conditions. We also provided strategies for competing with well-funded, VC-backed competitors by focusing on your unique strengths and delivering exceptional value to your customers. And we emphasized the importance of avoiding burnout and maintaining balance, prioritizing self-care and building a supportive network to help you weather the ups and downs of entrepreneurship.

Finally, we looked ahead to the long-term success and legacy of your bootstrapped business. We discussed how to grow sustainably by reinvesting your profits wisely and scaling your operations responsibly, balancing growth with profitability and planning for the long term. And we emphasized the importance of staying true to your original vision and values, building a business that is authentic, meaningful, and built to last.

Throughout this book, we've featured real-world examples and case studies of successful bootstrapped businesses across a range of industries, from software and e-commerce to consumer products and professional services. These stories serve as powerful reminders that building a thriving business without outside funding is not only possible, but increasingly common in today's entrepreneurial landscape.

We've also provided a wealth of practical resources and tools to help you along your journey, from templates for creating a lean business plan and tracking your financials, to recommended books, blogs, and communities for connecting with other bootstrappers and learning from their experiences.

But perhaps most importantly, we've aimed to provide you with the mindset, strategies, and inspiration you need to pursue your entrepreneurial dreams on your own terms. Bootstrapping a business is not for the faint of heart. It requires hard work, persistence, creativity, and a willingness to take calculated risks and learn from your mistakes. But for those who are up for the challenge, the rewards can be immense - not just financially, but in terms of the freedom, fulfillment, and impact you can create by building something truly remarkable from scratch.

So as you embark on your own bootstrapping journey, remember the key lessons and principles we've covered in this book. Stay focused on your purpose and your customers. Embrace a mindset of resourcefulness and adaptability. Surround yourself with a supportive network of mentors, peers, and partners. And most importantly, never lose sight of the unique vision and values that drove you to start your business in the first place.

Building a successful business without outside funding is not a linear or predictable path. There will be ups and downs, triumphs and setbacks, moments of doubt and moments of breakthrough. But with the right mindset, strategies, and support, you can navigate this journey with confidence and resilience, and emerge with a business and a legacy that you can be truly proud of.

So here's to you, the brave and determined bootstrappers who are forging your own paths and creating your own definitions of success. May this book serve as a valuable guide and companion on your journey, and may your businesses thrive and make a lasting positive impact on the world.

Thank you for reading "Bootstrapping Your Way to Success: Building a Business Without VC". We hope you've found it informative, inspiring, and practical, and we wish you all the best as you continue on your entrepreneurial journey. Remember, the world needs more bootstrappers like you - so keep dreaming big, starting small, and building something amazing.

Appendices

Tools:

1. Lean Canvas (leanstack.com/lean-canvas) - A one-page business plan template for quickly sketching out and testing business ideas.
2. Trello (trello.com) - A simple and flexible project management tool for tracking tasks, ideas, and progress.
3. Google Analytics (analytics.google.com) - Free web analytics for tracking and understanding your website traffic and user behavior.
4. Mailchimp (mailchimp.com) - An easy-to-use email marketing platform for building and engaging your audience.
5. QuickBooks (quickbooks.com) - Popular accounting software for managing your business finances and bookkeeping.
6. Stripe (stripe.com) - A payment processing platform for accepting online payments and subscriptions.
7. Zapier (zapier.com) - An automation tool for connecting your favorite apps and services to streamline your workflows.

8. Canva (canva.com) - A user-friendly graphic design tool for creating professional-looking images, logos, and marketing materials.
9. Typeform (typeform.com) - An online form and survey builder for gathering customer feedback and insights.
10. Notion (notion.so) - An all-in-one workspace for notes, docs, wikis, and project management.

Case Studies of Successful Bootstrapped Businesses

1. Buffer - A social media management platform that was bootstrapped to $10M in annual revenue before raising funding.
2. Braintree - A payment processing startup that was bootstrapped to $10M in revenue before being acquired by PayPal for $800M.
3. MailChimp - An email marketing platform that was bootstrapped for 17 years before reaching $600M in annual revenue.

4. Basecamp - A project management and team communication software that has been profitable since day one and generates over $25M in annual revenue.
5. Uncommon Goods - An online retailer of unique and creative gifts that was bootstrapped from a $15,000 investment to over $100M in annual revenue.
6. SimpliSafe - A home security startup that was bootstrapped for 8 years before raising a $57M round at a $600M valuation.
7. Grasshopper - A virtual phone system for small businesses that was bootstrapped to $30M in annual revenue before being acquired by Citrix.
8. Lynda.com - An online learning platform that was bootstrapped for 17 years before being acquired by LinkedIn for $1.5 billion.
9. Qualtrics - A survey and experience management software that was bootstrapped for 10 years before raising venture capital and eventually being acquired by SAP for $8 billion.
10. Tuft & Needle - A direct-to-consumer mattress startup that was bootstrapped to $100M in annual revenue before merging with Serta Simmons Bedding.

Templates for Lean Business Planning and Budgeting

Lean Business Plan Template:

1. Problem

- **Description:** What problem are you solving for your target customers?

2. Solution

- **Overview:** What is your proposed solution to the problem?

3. Key Metrics

- **Success Indicators:** What are the key metrics you will use to measure success?

4. Unique Value Proposition

- **Differentiation:** What makes your solution unique and better than competitors?

5. Unfair Advantage

- Competitive Edge: What gives you an unfair advantage in the market (expertise, network, technology, etc.)?

6. Channels

    - Customer Acquisition: What channels will you use to reach and acquire customers?

7. Customer Segments

    - Target Audience: Who are your target customers and what are their characteristics?

8. Cost Structure

    - Expenses: What are the key costs associated with running your business?

9. Revenue Streams

    - Monetization: How will you generate revenue and what are your pricing strategies?

Budget Template:

Category	Details	Amount ($)
Revenue		
	Product/Service 1	$X
	Product/Service 2	$X
	Total Revenue	**$X**
Expenses		
	Salaries and Wages	$X
	Employee Benefits	$X
	Marketing and Advertising	$X
	Rent and Utilities	$X
	Technology and Software	$X
	Professional Services (Legal, Accounting)	$X
	Office Supplies and Equipment	$X

	Travel and Entertainment	$X
	Insurance	$X
	Taxes and Licenses	$X
	Other Expenses	$X
	Total Expenses	**$X**
Net Profit	*(Revenue - Expenses)*	**$X**

Cash Flow

	Beginning Cash Balance	$X
	Cash Inflows (Revenue, Loans, Investments)	$X
	Cash Outflows (Expenses, Loan Payments, Distributions)	($X)
	Net Cash Flow	**$X**
	Ending Cash Balance	**$X**

Break-Even Analysis

	Fixed Costs (Rent, Salaries, etc.)	$X
	Variable Costs per Unit	$X
	Price per Unit	$X
	Break-Even Point (Units)	Fixed Costs ÷ (Price per Unit - Variable Costs per Unit)
	Break-Even Point (Sales)	Break-Even Point (Units) × Price per Unit

Sensitivity Analysis

Scenario 1	20% Increase in Sales	
	Revenue	$X
	Expenses	$X
	Net Profit	$X
Scenario 2	10% Increase in Costs	

	Revenue	$X
	Expenses	$X
	Net Profit	$X
Scenario 3	15% Decrease in Price	
	Revenue	$X
	Expenses	$X
	Net Profit	$X

Explanation of the Table:

- **Category**: Indicates the main section of the budget template (e.g., Revenue, Expenses, etc.).
- **Details**: Describes each line item within the category.
- **Amount ($)**: Placeholder for the monetary values.

Note: Be sure to customize these templates based on your specific business model, revenue streams, cost structure, and financial goals. Regularly review and update your plan and budget based on actual performance and changing market conditions. Consider working with a financial professional or mentor to refine your projections and strategies.

ABOUT THE AUTHOR

Harrell Howard is a prolific author and thought leader, specializing in a diverse array of subjects that cater to both personal and professional development. With a deep passion for empowering readers through knowledge, Harrell has penned numerous best-selling books, each offering practical insights and actionable strategies across various fields.

Harrell Howard combines a rich background in technology, marketing, and personal development to deliver content that is both insightful and practical.

When he's not writing, Harrell enjoys exploring new tech, market trends, and sharing his knowledge via speaking engagements and workshops. His drive for lifelong learning & passion for helping others is evident in his book.

www.ingramcontent.com/pod-product-compliance
Lightning Source LLC
Chambersburg PA
CBHW071022240526
45469CB00006BD/2041